HOME SAF

Home Safe Home

By
Helen Maxwell
With
Michael Maxwell, CPP

NEW HORIZON PRESS
Far Hills, New Jersey

Library of Congress Catalog Card Number: 92-60612

Helen Maxwell/Michael Maxwell
Home Safe Home

ISBN 0-88282-113-x
New Horizon Press

DEDICATED TO PAT CLEMENS

HOME SAFE HOME is an outgrowth of a crime. It is the authors' goal that the wealth of research they have gathered, regarding living defensively, may spare thousands of other people what she has had to experience as a result of an assailant's intrusion into her home.

Written with the cooperation of the Federal Bureau of Investigation, the International Association of Chiefs of Police, the Boston and Chicago Police Departments, the Los Angeles County Sheriff's Department, victim's advocacy groups, and Certified Protection Professionals recommended by the American Society for Industrial Security.

Acknowledgement

After the Los Angeles Riots, we decided to let twelve inner-city youths compete to do the illustrations for HOME SAFE HOME (LIVING DEFENSIVELY IN THE NINETIES). Joel Gomez was selected. Joel is seventeen years old and will be a senior in high school. He is a first-generation Mexican-American. His ambition is to be a professional illustrator.

Contents

Preface

Why is this book important to you and your family? To prevent trauma. Criminals are spoilers. They steal far more than possessions. What I discovered was that *after* a crime is over, the *real* adventure begins.

Victimization changes people forever. They may look the same, laugh at the same types of jokes, and prefer the same friends, but they will think differently after a crime. No matter how strong the person, there will be scars. According to psychologists who work with victims, those who have had their homes invaded *for* the commission of a crime often experience far more trauma than those who are victimized elsewhere. That safe feeling, the sense of privacy and the warmth of the "nest" is gone. It is my hope that through this book I may be able to spare many readers that loss.

The year I was victimized, I had come halfway across the country, leaving friends, a secure job, my church and familiar surroundings for a husband's career move. There is no good time for a crime to happen, although for me, this was a particularly bad time. I had no support system at my new home, my husband was extremely busy with the challenge of a new job, and my mother, who had always been there for support, was slipping into the final stages of Alzheimer's disease. That is the first lesson for readers. The victim does not get to choose the time a crime happens. Bad timing can destroy families and cause suicides, bankruptcy and divorce. Those consequences are factors assailants never think about. Once a crime is over, they go on to the next victim.

Before you read this book, it may help you to know, step by step, what a home intrusion is like. It is not like what you see on television. Crimes on television are over in an hour. But real crimes . . . well, those crimes leave an impact that lasts a long, long time.

While alone in the early hours of the morning, I awoke to a man's voice. I remember opening my eyes slowly and seeing a dark figure in the doorway of my bedroom, backlighted by the small nightlight in the hallway. I couldn't see features. The person spoke again. Still not totally awake, I thought it was my husband. I was confused. He wasn't supposed to be home. The voice said, "Where's the money?" The voice was not familiar. The person was in dark clothing, he was black, and he sounded cold and demanding. To him, I was a stranger, yet I detected hatred in his voice.

Like any woman alone, I next thought of my extremely vulnerable situation—I was alone in bed, and my husband was gone. I was wearing a low-cut, revealing nightgown. I had been a jogger for fifteen-years, running four to six miles a day. I was fit. I was large busted. I looked pretty good in those days. Terror flashed through my mind. They speak of the guilt of victims. That was the first grain of *my* guilt. I felt guilty about the way I was dressed. I felt guilty that my body was fit and might look tempting. I regretted that I was not flat-chested. It was silly to think those things, but I later learned it is fairly typical of victims.

What ensued was several hours of horror. He held a gun to my temple as I was walked around the house. My assailant turned lights on in front of slightly-opened curtains. He was bold and arrogant. He had torn up my living room prior to awakening me. He had torn up my kitchen. Things were all over the floor, papers were strewn about. It was alarming that he seemed more at home in my house than I did.

I had no weapon. I didn't like guns. Having the touch of a gun barrel against my head was almost more than I could bear. I worried, as I walked around, that he would trip, that his finger might slip and he would accidentally pull the trigger, that I would fall because I couldn't look down to get sure footing around so many objects he'd thrown on the floor. I didn't want to move my head, not a fraction of an inch.

I kept him busy, taking him to hiding place after hiding place where I had kept my valuables—my aunt's beautiful emerald ring. She had given it to me when she entered a rest home. He took it. I felt guilt. He took my diamond engagement ring. I asked for the guard bands, but he wouldn't let me keep them. He took my wedding ring, small family treasures from the drawers of my dressing table, another ring . . . a small amount of cash. I kept him busy so he wouldn't do what I feared most.

The night ended when I was told to stand in a corner and to turn around and face the wall. I knew my time with him was coming to a close. He had grabbed something . . . something made of fabric. I could barely see it out of the corner of my eye. He didn't tell me to put my hands behind my back for tying. I waited . . . I waited for what seemed a long, long time. I could smell him behind me. I felt I knew what was to happen. He was going to strangle me with what he had grabbed from the dirty clothes basket.

Chest pains hit me like knives piercing through my ribs. I have never known such pain. Vomit sputtered up in my throat. I crumbled instantly to the floor. He screamed at me to get up. I couldn't. He yelled again, but I was gasping for air; I couldn't inhale. For awhile, I thought my life was slipping away. I thought of all the things I hadn't yet been able to do. I thought of all the time I had wasted having a *perfectly* clean house. What would they say when I was gone? "She was such a good house-keeper."

I vowed that if I lived through this, I would put my priorities in balance. I panicked that I might not get the chance. There is no way to explain what it feels like to want to live when you think someone is going to kill you. A terrible feeling that life will soon be over and another person has total control.

After a long time—I don't know how much time had passed—I began to move again, to pull myself up. He had gone. For weeks I had severe bruises. I have no idea how I got them. I don't want to remember. When the police came they told me that the chest pains I had, at such a critical time, took the control of the crime out of my assailant's hands. The pains may have altered the route of the crime enough to save me.

They also told me he was a stalker; there was evidence he had been climbing a tree outside my second-story window. To get inside he had entered a living room window. The crime involved some terrible security design mistakes: a six-inch wide ledge on the first floor that allowed him to stand and pull himself up, vegetation that was like a jungle outside my front and side windows, weak window locks and more. I learned a lot that night.

But what came next was perplexing. I have since learned from a study by the Department of Psychiatry and Behavoral Medicine, Homewood Hospital Center; the John Hopkins Health System in Baltimore, Maryland; and the faculties of Harvard University; and Loyola College, also in Maryland; that Post Traumatic Stress Disorder is one of the *most under-rated and underdiagnosed of the major psychiatric clinical syndromes.* Many crime victims suffer from it. I was diagnosed as suffering from this malady.

If you are unlucky enough to be a crime victim, you may have the following symptoms: intrusive recollections of the crime; sudden feelings that the event is reoccurring due to association with similar environmental stimuli; reduced involvement with the external world; diminished interest in significant activities; feelings of estrangement; hyperalertness; exaggerated startle response (I still have that symptom badly.); sleep disturbance; guilt, memory impairment; avoidance of any activity associated with the crime; difficulty concentrating.

It was once thought that only war, combat situations, produced those symptoms. Due to the victim's movement, coupled with the progressivism of the psychology community in this country, Post Traumatic Stress Disorder in crime victims is now "real." It is being taken seriously, and crime victims are getting treatment. If you know a victim of a crime, realize that the crime may be over for *you* once you hear of it. For the victim, the struggle is often just beginning.

After the intrusion into my home, I started to build on my journalism background and began researching the many factors that contributed to my being targeted for a home break-in. I read all of Joseph Wambaugh's books in one week to better understand police. I became a good friend of a female deputy sheriff in my neighborhood. I learned that big city police officers (and I'm sure, others as well) are remarkably intelligent people who see things we never even notice in our environments. Many are keen thinkers, educated, and extremely street-smart. I was fascinated. I read about sociology and about investigations. Eventually, I took a five-part exam to be a crime prevention specialist. I passed with a 97.6 score. The test was difficult. I was proud.

Through the years that followed, my interest and knowledge of crime, security and police continued to grow. I studied; I wrote. I administered a college certified, police science education program. I have been told by law enforcement people I respect that I am now considered an expert on this subject. I'm not sure that is true. In this field, if you miss one week of study, you are not an expert. However, I have written for "inside" police publications on everything from gang interdiction to police response in times of crisis. I think, perhaps, these writings may have saved some lives.

After the traumatic weeks following my crime, one thing made a strong impact on me. That is, how weak the resources are for victims who want to lesson the odds that they will be victims again. I read personal security books that "spoke" to me, as if I were an electrician or a veteran carpenter. I am neither, and they didn't help me. I read books and articles that focused totally on the barricade mentality. I now know murderers, rapists, thieves and gangmembers. I also know some of the finest police managers and patrol officers. I have interviewed many on both sides of the law to learn more about this subject. I spent months gaining the confidence of a man in maximum security so I could ask . . . "O. K., Dennis, so you raped nine women, how did you choose them, and tell me how you got into those houses." I have learned that the barricade mentality is *not* the best way to fight crime. Security equipment is only part of this book.

If you want to install your own alarm system (I don't recommend it.), this is not the book for you. If you want to be a knowledgable consumer before choosing an alarm system, there is no better information than what my experts have provided. If you want advice from Certified Protection Professionals; if you would like to read what the International Association of Chiefs of Police has to say about whether you should own a gun; if you want to know the FBI predictions of what dangers are over the horizon or how security can be tailored to your "Golden Years" or for young children, read this book.

Finally, most books on technical subjects are dry. Well . . . OK, my chapter on alarms isn't going to give you goosebumps, but I think you will be fascinated by a lot of what you are going to read. You don't think fences and walls can be interesting? They can, when the United States Marines test their effectiveness. I have tried to make this self-help book fun to read so the ideas on the pages will stay with you. I thank the Federal Bureau of Investigation (San Francisco and Los Angeles offices), the International Association of Chiefs of Police, and the California Office of the Attorney General, for their assistance in gathering information for this book. And, most of all, I thank Michael Maxwell, a Certified Protection Professional and a police executive himself, for his support and supreme knowledge in combing through the pounds of information I collected nationally for this very ambitious endeavor.

· 1 ·

Police and Burglars

On April 26, 1992, FBI Director William Sessions announced that crime has continued to rise since 1985. Violent crime rose 5 percent in 1991, as compared to 1990. According to FBI statistics, the number of burglaries from January through December 1991 were: 10,048 in Albuquerque, 50,203 in Chicago, 32,975 in Dallas, 119,937 in New York City, and 16,580 in Memphis. The number of murders, assaults and rapes within homes were equally staggering.

If you have been a victim, or you know someone who has been a victim, you already have learned why living defensively is important. Anytime, anywhere, you may be someone's prey. But, according to psychologists who work with victims, being a victim in your own home brings the most trauma. Your home is where you are supposed to feel relaxed, content—safe. After your home is invaded, *nowhere* feels safe.

Most books on home security involve the academic approach to living defensively. Most authors of those books *are* academics. Though much of the information disseminated on living defensively is good information, it often is presented dryly by authors who have never known criminals, or who have not experienced day-to-day relationships with police in extremely busy law enforcement agencies. *Nothing* . . . no amount of research, graphs or diagrams can take the place of what both police officers *and* criminals gain from their very colorful careers. It is *street-savvy*. Once a person has gained street-savvy, he or she has insight into how burglars, rapists or armed robbers think and gain an edge on living defensively. All the locks, high fences and steel doors you put on a home cannot protect a person who retains a victim's mentality—a naivete.

For that reason, the first chapter of this book is possibly the most important. You are going to meet Detective Steve Rubino of the Los Angeles County Sheriff's Department, Richard Doyle of the Boston Police Department, and "Charlie," a female career criminal touted by the undercover detective who finally caught her as an extremely successful burglar. When you complete this chapter, all other chapters in this book will fall easily into place. Hopefully, you will have gained at least a shred of street-smarts and will be able to see better the world from a criminal's eyes.

HOW VULNERABLE
ARE YOU?

Detective Steve Rubino, Los Angeles County
Sheriff's Department

Steven Rubino works undercover in the highly specialized Multi-Jurisdictional Criminal Apprehension Detail, called MCAD. MCAD investigators have a unique view of career criminals. Unlike most police officers who are reactive and come upon scenes *after* crimes have occurred, MCAD detectives are told *before* a crime, and they frequently watch the crime being initiated. Most of MCAD's suspects are burglars and armed robbers, and Steve Rubino follows them from the time they get up in the morning until they go home at night.

"MCAD gains information on burglars and armed robbers from people on the streets," Rubino explains. "Heroin addicts, people in jail who have information and want to make deals. We get the names. Then we find out where the suspects live and where they hang out. When they start their day, we're there." When a house burglary occurs, MCAD moves in.

"What a burglar does is he drives through the neighborhood to pick a house. Burglars don't like dogs, they don't like noise. They'll park down the street from the house they choose, then they'll go up and knock on the door. They wait. If no one answers, they'll go to the rear of the house, find a spot and break in. The dumb burglars will go through the front door.

"What if someone is home, when they knock on the door? They'll say something like . . . I'm looking for Joey. Is Joey home?" According to Rubino, "Ninety-nine percent of the time, if a stranger comes to your door and asks for someone you've never heard of, he's a burglar looking for a hit. Get his license number, call the police." According to Rubino's experience following burglars on the West Coast, *most* commit their entries before one o'clock in the afternoon while residents are at work.

"Nighttime burglars are far more dangerous than daytime burglars," Rubino says. "Nighttime burglars know people are at home. Nighttime burglars are usually armed. If they wake people up, they are prepared to get violent. Nighttime burglars are also more cautious and more sophisticated. They are smarter. They wear gloves and dark clothing, they anticipate trouble. And they anticipate running into the police.

"A burglar will usually use a screwdriver or a crowbar that he carries concealed under his shirt," Rubino says. "I've seen them use pliers. These days, a lot of intruders have no qualms about breaking glass to get in. I had a guy who did 50 residential burglaries . . . apartments, and he went the easy way, through false ceilings in the hallways. A resident would hear a noise and look up to see legs coming down from his ceiling. For people who park their cars in front of the house, we had two kids who had stolen over 150 Honda Preludes. These guys were cranking with a screwdriver or a dent puller. On another series of cases, we had a female burglar who hit two or three homes a night. Not all burglars are men. Although when a woman works 'burgs,' she usually works with a man. She is usually the driver."

If the burglary rate seems excessively high, all the burglary investigators interviewed for this book cited one reason—drugs. "The number of crimes a burglar commits depends on how much dope he is using," Rubino says. "The burglary rate is directly linked to the nation's drug problem." (A burglary victim who awakens to find an intruder in the home should not forget that factor. Today's burglars are often desperate.) "If a burglar has a real bad habit, he'll be going out every night. He has to, just to keep the habit going. How often he goes out also depends on how much he gets for the stolen property."

Should you fear being murdered during a burglary? The answer is yes. "We did a search warrant on a case," Rubino says, "where the woman came home to find a burgler in her house. He stabbed her. She made it out to the yard and he stabbed her again while she was helpless on the ground. He wanted to kill her. He didn't want a witness."

Burglars can even fool MCAD. Once, Rubino's team had a pair of burglars under surveillance. They entered one yard, only to hit a neighboring house while the MCAD team sat waiting. "All the stolen property came over a fence. When they pulled out their truck was loaded with stuff. A lot of burglars are smart, but eventually they all slip up."

Sergeant Richard Doyle, Boston Police Department

Sergeant Richard Doyle has been with the Boston Police Department for 26 years. His grandfather was a policeman in 1909; his father started his police career in 1941. Doyle's brother is also a police officer. If anyone has been saturated with knowledge about crime and criminals, it is Sergeant Doyle. He has much to share.

In the city of Boston, all information regarding stolen property is entered into a computer. The read-out automatically compares this list against property pawned at pawn shops and second-hand dealers. Any item sold has to be held for thirty days. A written report of the seller and a description of the item has to be furnished to the police within twenty-four hours. Not all cities do this.

This process keeps a running tab on suspicious individuals. "You'd have an individual going in and selling two women's rings one day," Sergeant Doyle explains. "The next day he'd go in and sell three men's rings. Then he'd go in the next day and sell a violin, then a watch. It's people like that we would target. Or we'd have a person giving a drug dealer a five-thousand dollar violin for drugs. Our burglary task force ending up doing a lot of drug investigations because of the link between burglary and drugs. Doyle recalled one career burglar who was so successful that the Oriental community in one Boston neighborhood took out a "contract" on him. "He picked his victims carefully," Doyle says. "He watched them. Then he'd tie a rope to a chimney and he'd go right down the side of a ten-story building and into a window. He'd use a real cheesy rope, like clothesline. He only hit Orientals' homes. He knew the Oriental people didn't trust banks and also didn't trust police. So with that combination, they didn't even report a lot of the crimes. One 'snitch' told us he took sixty-thousand dollars from one house alone. *Everybody* knew who he was . . . the snitches and the neighbors. Nobody would come forward. The neighborhood finally put a contract out on him. An old crime family, a 'shooter,' was coming in from out of town. We saved his life when we put him in jail on drug charges."

Aside from this memorable case, Doyle says, "Rehabs can be very bad burglary risks. Those are large commercial buildings or larger apartments broken into smaller living units. Some contractors do a slip-shod job," Doyle says. "When they start splitting them up, all they do is put in a hollow plasterboard hallway. You can actually punch a hole in the wall with your fist, reach around and unlock a door. Frequently, the landlords buy the cheapest locks they can get, and the lease says you can't change the locks."

The most successful burglar works during the day, according to Doyle. And the pro's target certain neighborhoods over others. "In Boston, we have the Roxbury area. It is not affluent. If you break in there, you might get a stereo or TV. But if you move a quarter of a mile away to Hyde Park, or go to the South End, you have a lot of business people who have paid a million to a million-and-a-half for a gutted tenement that they've rebuilt. That's where burglars get good stuff. I could take you down an area there and you could knock on every door on the street. If you found two people at home in the daytime, you'd be lucky." It's a high target for home intrusion.

"I had a burglar who had done a lot of burglaries," Doyle recalled. "He told me that his father was a thief . . . a burglar too. He said his father always taught him, 'Don't steal anything you can't carry in your pocket.' Because once you're out on the street, there is no way anyone can detect what you've done. You look like 150,000 other people. But, if you're carrying a television set or a pillowcase with something in it, you will pique my curiosity. This guy would go right in and take money and jewelry. Stick it in his pocket. That's all he stole. He wouldn't touch a television set for the world. He rarely got busted. He said his father was only busted a couple of times."

It is also Doyle's experience that usually a burglar will go to the front door and knock. "They'll have books in their hand, anything that makes it look like they're selling something. If no one is around, they'll go around to the back, force their way in. Apartment houses? It's usually the front door. Bing . . . you're in. It's very easy to get into apartment buildings. Somebody is always waiting to get in at the front door buzzer. Somebody always lets the intruder in."

Doyle says that burglars usually sell what they've stolen the next day. "Defending yourself against home intruders, burglars, is all common sense," Doyle says. "Realizing that there are people out there who want what you have. You just have to be a little bit smarter than they are."

2

Meet the Enemy

"Charlie" is white, clean-scrubbed and attractive, with shoulder-length, light brown hair. She has worked as a secretary and as an assistant in an "up-scale" health spa. Charlie looks like the girl next door—only Charlie is a career criminal, a burglar and a dope dealer. She claims she tired of working for low pay and was weary of constant struggle. Her mother is a stripper, and her father has had drug and alcohol problems. She became a drug user through experimentation at a party. The drug use escalated. Charlie, who is now a mother herself, is part of an underworld, a city within a city, with different values than yours and unforgiving ways.

The first lesson in street-savvy is that career criminals aren't always like television villains . . . not all are one-dimensional and mean. Many are quite likeable. In many ways, they are like you. They could be your neighbor, your friend with a secret life, someone you date or the freckle-faced teenager down the block. Only most burglars usually have drug habits, and they cross lines to maintain that lifestyle. Some burglars steal for the "kick" or because they are too lazy to do regular work. The professionals relish the challenge of their jobs.

Charlie is going to tell you how she committed over 250 car and house burglaries in only 90 days, as confirmed by the undercover investigator who caught her. And she will tell you why she prefers this life to any other.

"CHARLIE"

"I started burglarizing to make money to support a drug habit. I had all the money I wanted, and I had all the drugs. I had everything. It (burglarizing) turned out to be for the thrill of it all. It was a thrill.

"The easiest house to burgle? A fumigated house. I love 'em' *I love 'em.* I see those tents, and I'm on my way. Consider me *in* that house. You just assume they're (residents) not in there. If they were in there, they're gonna die. (laughs) So, I get a gas mask on . . . my co-defendent got me that. That was a clever little idea. If your eyes start to water, you got goggles.

"It's tricky to get in there, though. You gotta' crawl underneath. And you can't turn on lights because people will see 'em. Can't turn on lights. So I worked with a flashlight.

"You don't cut your way in. That might arouse suspicion. You just got to pull underneath. It all depends on which fumigating company. You got to pull the tarp. It sometimes snaps. You got to crawl under. I've crawled under many garages (garage doors). You just got to learn to suck it in.

"You target your houses. 'Course, you look to see how many newspapers are out front. My thing was. . . . I was hip on credit cards. You should tell the people in your book that when they go to check their wallets. . . . 'cause I was the type of person that would get into a car. Find the garage door opener, open the garage. Walk away for an hour. Make sure they didn't wake up. Come back an hour later if they weren't awake.

"Boy, I found a brand new Jaquar with the keys in it. With a purse. I didn't take it though. You go into the purse and you take *one* credit card. I work basically up in Palos Verdes. The people up there are so filthy rich, they don't check. They usually have gold cards. All unexpired. All ready to use. You take one, you leave everything else there. They're not going to notice.

"If you want to know the truth, we would drive up and down in other counties. We'd drive around, looking for open garages. I'd start about midnight and work until about six in the morning. My co-defendent had some guts. He had some heart. 'Cause he'd go into houses with people still sleeping. I wouldn't do it. But he would. If there is a dog there, dogs are number one. Got to watch out for those dogs. God, those dogs.

"My weapons? A flashlight. Screwdriver. Underneath the seat, we had boltcutters. Always had a scanner. Had a 200 channel pro-gram-able. Ooooo. But I got that illegally too! You have the scanner on; know what the cops are doing.

"I went into this one house, I took antiques. This man had Pony Express days mail locks. Pony Express days. Ooooh, damn. And machetes. Big machetes. And guns. From the British Army. And his wife had coats. And they had crystal. Waterford crystal. I spent all night in that house. I spent *all* night in that house. They weren't home . . . they were fumigating! I was walking around . . . carting that stuff out all night long. Never got caught. Never got caught. Yeah . . . I was good, wasn't I? But, burglaries weren't my cup of tea. I dealt drugs. Meth . . . speed.

"The burglaries started out as trashing. Going out and digging in trashes. Just to see what we could find. When you're on speed, you do wierd things. We'd go and we'd hunt in trashes. It went on to getting a flashlight and look-ing in cars. Seeing those Raybans. I *had* to have them. And it got bigger, and bigger, and bigger.

"(Getting into cars) Ninety percent were open. Some were at homes. I liked the . . . uh . . . the uh . . . where you have the condominiums, where you have carports? I like those, because it's not a personal garage. Usually, you drive up to garages, and see, the cars are all right there. You don't have to walk from house to house to house. When do people leave their garages open? Trust me, they do. All over the place.

"Did I feel guilty? Yeah . . . afterwards. I felt guilty 'cause I got caught. I'm not going to lie about it. *I felt guilty 'cause I got caught.*

"There was a lot of times, I'd go in garages. I'd find their car keys, and take them. That was it. Leave their garage. Write down the address, go back later when no one was home. Open the door. No forceable entry. They never knew I was there. A lot of people are careless with their car keys. I could have taken their whole car. A lady with a Mercedes, I could have taken her whole Mercedes . . . everything. I opened up her trunk and found her brand new Sony handicam. I took that. Yeah, I took that.

"I'd say I did one house every other night . . . and, *at least* forty car burglaries a night. At least.

"I'd go from car to car to car. I'd usually get in. Car alarms? Aaaah, I got wise to those. My co-defendent taught me all I needed to know about those. The car alarms—very rarely are they used. The blinking red lights, a lot of times, if you pay attention, the blinking red lights are for the *radio* alarm, if somebody tries to take a radio.

"We did cut the alarms off, sometimes. All you have to do is reach up, grab the battery cable and pull. Some are better than that. Some are high technology. Some are smarter than me. So, if it goes off, you just high-tail it.

"Unless there is something really bad in that car, I'd go to the next car. But, usually, at one point, I had to have that purse. *Had to have it.* And I got it, too. Took a tire iron, smashed the window, the alarm went off, grabbed the purse . . . smash and grab . . . ran . . . dogs barking. But, I got two ATM cards with pin numbers. The pin numbers were right next to the ATM cards. And there were two people on each card. So I got two-hundred, two-hundred, two-hundred and two-hundred. Just went from 7-11, to 7-11, to 7-11, to 7-11.

"House alarms. I ran into some of those. But there's no getting over those. You just high-tail it, 'cause you know the police will be close by, soon.

(Charlie boasts that her best burglarizing was in Palos Verdes/Rancho Palos Verdes, California.) "Oooooh, yes. They pay for their own police department. Yes, they do. You should see . . . we set off car alarms, sat there and watched the police department circulate. I was in someone's back yard. We sat there, ducking and dodging them, in these people's backyard . . . watching the cops circulate. They had us. We were pinned. Lomita Sheriff's Station got me. A snitch got taken to jail the day before I got busted.

"For burglaries, I'd dress all dark. Sweats. Can't wear tight pants. I was caught wearing white that night. I was all in white. Don't ask me why . . . I was feeling off that day. I had a feeling something was going to happen.

" 'Burgs' are like going to Disneyland every night. Once that is in your blood, it's hard to stop. Yeah, it would be hard to work as a secretary and not make decent money. Not 'caper.' You can't. 1994 comes, watch out . . . (Denotes end of her prison sentence. She laughs.) I'm joking. I'm joking.

(Charlie was asked how committing burglaries compared with other pursuits in her life.) "At that time in my life? The burglaries fell second. First, was my dope. Drugs. I couldn't have done the burglaries without my drugs. It would take the edge off, the thrill of it.

"I didn't want to get caught. It was a thrill being high. It was a thrill in itself. If you ever meet anybody else who burglarizes like I did, ask them what drugs they do. I betcha I know what drug they do. Methamphetamine . . . that's it. I felt like I had the world by the tail. That's it.

"I told my co-defendent time after time after time . . . we came close to being caught . . . got pulled over with purses in the car. There were two of them. (Police officers.) We were doing 'em, we were right there, doing 'em. (Burglaries.) And I had this lady's purse.

"I had it (the loot) all at my feet, and it was stuck in the back. And these cops came up. And they said, 'We just got a phone call.' Shining lights on me. We were parked. Eric said, 'Officer' . . . we get out of the car. I gave them a bogus name. Charlene Montgomery. And he said, 'Come over here.' He separated us.

"I heard Eric tell him, 'We're having car trouble, Officer. We *cannot* start the car.' I saw the cop look inside the car. (makes motion of searching with light) Going like this. He said, 'What's all this shit in the car?'

"I said, 'Officer, listen to me. He don't know what he's saying. Check this out . . . (pauses and congratulates herself at duping police.) I'm good. *That's* my boyfriend. We just had a fight. He's an idiot. He doesn't know what he's saying. He's an asshole. He brought me here. I think he's a jerk. You know . . . we're sitting there fighting, this car won't start. This girl who was in the car with him earlier, left all of this stuff here, (giggles) We got away with it. He said, 'Get in your car and go.'

"That's just the way it is. The only people I know who didn't burglarize, were my family. I mean, we had a whole caravan of people going out and doing it. None of them had jobs. They did burglaries.

Charlie gives advice to potential victims): "What to do to their houses? What would I tell them? Get a garage door opener. Make sure their outside light is always on. *Always.* I didn't like to mess with houses with lights. The garage door opener is the main one. Because I got into a lot of houses through the garage. You open up the garage, make sure your car doors are locked. It's the standard stuff they just don't listen to. When you're a kid, people say, 'Don't do this, don't do that.' But, you don't do it. Lock your car up. If it helps, get one of those little blinky lights, 'cause they sure got me for awhile. But, I got over those. I got over those. Get a blinky light. My co-defendent had one in his car, and there was no car alarm whatsoever.

"Dogs . . . dogs. Dogs are a big help. But, a lot of people have dog doors? *Big* misunderstanding with those dog doors. You just reach your hand up, and you can get into that house. It only has to be about that big of a dog door (she holds out her hand, about 18 inches high). You stretch. When I got busted . . . ooooh, when I got busted, I had bruises, right here. From reaching in windows. This is through car windows that I got the bruises. Through doors, all you got to do is reach up and stretch. It takes awhile. I was dealing dope before I did this. God, I was having the time of my life. I could have still been there at South Shores living in a nice house by the sea.

(Charlie was asked if she would steal from people she knew.) "Uh . . . people I knew and *liked?* Just knew? Yeah, I would if I didn't like them."

(Is burglarizing hard work?) "Yeah, it was. You're darn tootin' it is. You have to be smart to do it. This is how I look at it. I'm twenty-three. I had to outsmart a man (the detective) who went to college, went to all these things. I had to outsmart them all. They all *knew* me. I had to outsmart them all. They're good. But, they're not as good as me. And I could do it again, too. And this time, they wouldn't catch me. Because I'm *better.*"

3

Crime Statistics in Your City

DON'T BE LULLED INTO A FALSE SENSE OF SECURITY BY NUMBERS

One major lesson learned in any statistics class is this . . . "Numbers say what you want them to say." This bit of wisdom is true no matter who is gathering the numbers, analyzing them, publishing them, or using them to prove a point. Granted, numbers can be a great source of information, necessary to formulate positions and expenditures, but they also can bolster *any* point of view—regarding crime rates.

While researching this book, we happened to inquire of a major police agency about the number of burglaries for 1991. "Why," we were told, "we don't have a significant burglary rate here. Our burglary rate is WAY DOWN, thanks to our proactive patrol and excellent police management." This claim was difficult to accept, especially since ALL cities in the area of the size of this one had reported a sharp increase in residential burglaries. Further probing revealed that the reason this city didn't have a "significant burglary rate" was that no burglaries had been reported. Burglary was not classified as a crime in this city. Statistics revealed only a sharp increase in related crimes, such as trespassing and petty theft, necessary elements of the felony of burglary. It's all in how you spell it.

If an agency wants to make people believe that nightime burglaries have decreased, it is only necessary to adjust the hours reported as "nightime." For instance, let's assume the agency included in the category "nightime burglaries," all burglaries occurring between the hours of 6:00 PM and 6:00 AM. To give the impression that nightime burglaries decreased, it is a simple matter of altering the requirements of "nightime burglary." All the agency has to do is decrease the amount of time covered, re-categorizing the "nightime burglaries" as those burglaries occurring between the hours of 10:00 PM and 4:00 AM, a loss of six hours of reporting time. Easy.

A way to increase the crime numbers, to scare the population, or justify additional allocation of funds for new police officers or equipment, is to saturate a low-crime patrol district for a certain reporting period. The amount of crime will not increase, but the amount of REPORTED crime will increase, since there are more police officers in the area for citizens to report them to, to see crimes being committed, and to take reportable police action. Crime didn't increase, but the number of crime reports jumped due to increased police activity.

Another way to skew crime statistics is to alter slightly the definition of the crime. Say, instead of defining rape as forcible sexual intercourse, or an attempt at forcible sexual intercourse, the agency re-defines it as "forcible sexual intercourse, not including attempts" and fails to report those attempts at "forcible rape." All of a sudden, the numbers of "rapes" is down, lulling the local population into a false sense of security. All the while, the number of rapes has not decreased, but the numbers of re-defined "rapes" has dropped. Watch those numbers . . . get the facts on any sudden or unexplained increase or decrease in crimes.

Why would someone want to cloud crime statistics, to make them what they aren't? Look for skewed crime statistics during election years prior to local or county bond issues, the hiring of a new chief of police (or the firing of an old one), or to justify increases in pay or equipment costs.

· 4 ·

Security Landscaping,
Not Always Obvious

Landscape design can serve as an invitation to a home intruder. Though crime prevention officers from local police departments may criticize the height of your hedges or the vine that leads to an upstairs bedroom, security landscaping is far more complex than that. The rich can afford landscape architects, which in most states require state licenses. Landscape architects, because of their wealthy clientele, are usually expert in plant use, both for its beauty *and* its impact on security. One of the best, is Dan Weedon, who works the "high-end" neighborhoods of Beverly Hills, Brentwood and Bel Aire in Los Angeles County. Although most middle income homeowners cannot afford Weedon, many elements of his expertise can benefit the average homeowner. By rule of thumb, a four-hundred-thousand dollar house will cost forty-thousand dollars to landscape, or ten-percent of the cost of the home. As the cost of the home rises, the cost of the landscaping ceases to climb, unless there are unusual requirements. Beverly Hills, where Weedon does much of his work, is a city with strict regulation on security features. If all cities had the rules currently on the books in Beverly Hills, homeowners would be safer.

"When focusing on security," Weedon says, "most people think of gates, walls and security equipment . . . cameras and so on. But, there is a lot of plant material that has its own armor, that can augment anything built or installed to further secure a property."

In Beverly Hills, residents cannot have front yard fences or gates over six-feet high. Many up-scale neighborhoods have such rules, primarily for aesthetic reasons. Residents don't want their neighborhoods to look like armed camps. However, plants can grow much taller than six-feet, and Weedon uses them to augment the height of the fences and gates. "If the plants have thorns or sticky flowers," he says, "it further enhances security."

Many municipalities have rules requiring that nothing obstruct the front of a home to give police a clear view of the property. That is true in Beverly Hills. Plants can increase security, but they can also hinder security if police or security patrols cannot see an intruder behind your high brick walls.

For the security of its residents, the City of Beverly Hills does not allow solid fences over three-feet high at the front of a property. If a barrier is added above a solid fence, it must be constructed of wrought iron or materials that allow police to view the premises, in case a home intrusion were underway. If iron fencing is used, no more than 50 percent of the hedges or vines may obscure the view.

Weedon points out that security and privacy, often related, are two different things. Most of his clients are concerned about privacy. Tour vans are still allowed to drive through Beverly Hills neighborhoods. Maps are sold to celebrities' homes. Clients want vines and hedges, not for security, but for privacy.

The newest security focus in many cities is toward citizen activism—getting city governments to close off streets and to post gates and guards. Such limitation of public access is bringing new problems. Why should only the affluent get to do this? With crime increasing, Weedon claims that more and more neighborhoods will become small villages behind walls and gates.

However, plants in themselves can deny access to your property. "The ones with thorns and stickers will tear you up," Weedon says. "And there is a broad variety of cactus. Cactus will grow faster, given more water than a desert provides. But, cactus won't lend itself to lush landscape, which many homeowners prefer. Lush plants can provide security in a less painful way because of their density. They are difficult for an intruder to get through. Travel takes more time, more struggle. There are plants you would need a machete to get through. Bamboo, for instance."

Plant communities vary greatly, depending upon where in the United States you live. In California and in other tropical states, a vast botanic garden can grow easily. From San Diego to Santa Barbara, and inland about fifteen-miles in Southern California, 95 percent of the plant material available on the planet is available for horticulture use. There are few regions in the world where such a variety of plantlife can be used for security landscaping. It's a little more complicated in other parts of the country, where fewer plants thrive due to harsh winters.

A problem for many city dwellers is a backyard area that slopes down to a freeway or a well-travelled street. Regardless of having a fenced-in area or a guard at the entrance to a secured community, a prowler can still crawl up the slope. To solve this problem for the Sultan of Brunei, reputed at the time to be the richest man in the world, Weedon secured the slope with plants. Since the land was not stable, and too much water would cause it to collapse, plants needing regular watering could not be used. Only draught-tolerant natives to Southern California, requiring only the water that fell from the sky were considered. Bougainvillea, which is an excellent screen and a barrier as well, was first choice.

Bougainvillea is only two to three feet tall, but according to Weedon, as a security barrier it is all that is needed. Each plant spreads approximately three feet. The thorns of a mature plant grow to three inches long. Bougainvillea looks beautiful on a slope, yet it is an excellent passive security measure. If Bougain-villea won't thrive in your part of the United States, plants that are dense, even if they have no thorns, retard a prowler's progress, or may keep him out of your property entirely.

Regarding the liability issue and the damage thorns can do to an intruder, Weedon claims never to have heard of such a problem. "A guard dog is more obvious," he says. "If a dog is snarling at you, and you go into the property anyway? Thorns can be a surprise. It's like climbing over a spiked fence, falling and injuring yourself. Common sense says you shouldn't have been there, although people seem to sue over anything." (Consult the chapter on liability for a tort expert's analysis of vegetation used for security.)

According to Weedon, residents of Palm Springs use olean-der as a barrier. Mature oleander bushes are so dense a person would have to hack his way through. Weedon claims to use vegetation that is far lower in cost than the price of a fence and that certain plants do a better job than a fence can do. "And it will look nicer than a fence," he says.

In Beverly Hills, there is a regulation that no fences on back alleys may be higher than eight feet. A hedge can be planted that will reach fifteen to twenty feet. Residents who are insistent on that level of privacy, do it. Normally, a landscape architect will combine a fence *with* a hedge. The problem is, plantlife cannot provide security right away. Plants have to grow. In the meantime, the fence is relied upon until the plants mature. A chained-link fence is an excellent, though inelegant security feature. Vines can be planted along it. The plants' tentacles will grow through the holes in the fence, until eventually the fence will not show, at all. Even if you have a pair of wirecutters, according to Weedon, and you try to disconnect the links, the vines will have grown so thick that it will be extremely difficult even to get to the fence. The fence ends up serving as a backdrop, a net, to the dense hedge, and is excellent for security.

"Normally, in my experience with security companies, we end up butting heads," Weedon says. "They are running photoelectric cells, free-sight lines. They don't want leaves breaking the beams. They will put sensors on the fences, and they don't want plants growing in there, pulling on the wires. We usually work things out."

Many architects think in terms of, "I want that high wall." Weedon says landscape architects are brought in to make things look right, to look pleasing. "A lot of technical security features are fine, but why make them look like hell?" he says. One problem can be that the security consultant decides on three cameras. He doesn't want to go over budget. If there are to be trees or shrubs in the way, he may have to put in more cameras. Many times, landscape architects will relocate trees for security's sake. If full-sized trees are brought in, the cameras can be hidden in the trees. Then, the homeowner doesn't have to have a pole in the middle of the yard, and all those wires."

Regarding the safety of a pool area, landscape designers are frequently asked to secure a pool, without making it look like a cage. Landscaping and fencing are designed in such a way that they are unobtrusive. Small gates are bypassed for large gates that swing out of the way. Vegetation is cleverly integrated into the design. As an added safety feature, there are beams that sense motion on the water, in case someone hops over your fence at night and goes for a swim. Jacuzzis create problems, if you want to use a pool cover to deter "guests." If you desire a fountain, there are fountain designs with only an inch of water. Cobbles fill the fountain. When children are older, the cobbles are taken out.

Every burglary detective has run onto cases where the burglar or home intruder used a tree to get to the second floor of a home. There are some trees that are dangerous to climb. They are brittle and the limbs are likely to break under human weight. But, that can be a liability too. The limbs can break and fall on someone's car. They can break while a child is climbing the tree. The Chorisa trunk is covered with giant thorns. "You wouldn't want to get near one," Weedon says. "But I don't use them on property where their might be children or pets running around. If you fell on a Chorisa, you would be seriously hurt. They are beautiful trees. The trunks are fat and are bright green. Bright pink flowers bloom in the spring and summer, and the trees can get sixty-feet tall. But, they won't take freezing temperatures or cold weather."

On the east coast and in the midwest, according to Weedon, landscape architects are limited to fifteen to twenty plants for security design. There are strict limits to what can be done with security landscaping. In those parts of the country, it is best to focus on density of vegetation—plant materials that make it difficult for humans to move through. Evergreens would be Weedon's first choice.

If you decide to use plants to enhance your home security, and you can't afford a landscape architect, consider approaching a university that has landscape architectural programs. There are many students who will take jobs merely for the experience. It is best to choose a student in his or her senior year. Approach the chairperson of that department and suggest that your yard be a class project. Suddenly, there is only the cost of the plants. You may get thirty plans from which to choose.

Landscape architects will come to your home and evaluate your grounds. Make your security needs known. If after reading this book, you can't decide what your security needs are, pay for a consultation. Make sure the person is a Certified Protection Professional. If no CPP's are available in your area, consult your police agency's crime prevention specialist for suggestions.

Next, the landscape architect—a student or a veteran in the profession—will go through a list of plants with you, and they will oversee the planting, finally giving you advice on the maintenance of your investment. If you can afford the real thing, you can write the National Association of Architects in Washington, DC for a list of architects in your area. Your local library should be able to provide you with the list.

Finally, in the *Sunset Western Garden Book* (Lane Publishers) hedges, screens and barrier plants are listed, with designations on climate zones. Those plants indicated as barriers are described as "impenetrably dense, armed with thorns or both."

Plants recommended as barriers are: berberis, bamboo, carissa, liex, juniperus (columnar varieties), juniperus (shrubs), mahonia aquifolium mahonia nevinii, melaleuca armillaris, pyracantha, and ribes speciosum. Consult your local nursery to determine which vegetation thrives in your climate.

Contact your local nursery, the larger the better, for availability of plant materials best suited for *your* area. The region in which you live may support plant species not on the published list.

If there are no landscape architects near where you live, you may consult a large nursery or a landscape business for help with your security landscaping; but consider that these businesses will be in a direct conflict of interest. They will *sell* you the plants. A landscape architect takes bids on the plants and makes sure you are not gouged.

Should you turn to a gardener for security landscaping advice? Weedon says you shouldn't. "It used to be, that there were *real* gardeners. They knew plants, they knew how to take care of them. And they had training and experience. Most of the people now seem to be 'blow and go' people. It's a guy with a pick-up truck and a lawnmower—hack jobs. Too many of them don't know what they are doing." Weedon says he is frequently brought in to do assessments of damage, wrought "by these people." Lawsuits. "What would it cost to replace this tree? Weedon will obtain photographs of what the tree looked like before. "A person can spend forty to fifty-thousand dollars to landscape a place, and this guy will come in, and in one month he has killed everything. During the Eighties, there was a move to license gardeners, but with the emphasis on deregulation, the movement didn't get far." The right people to maintain your security landscaping may cost more, but they will spot insects that are a problem, they will know how to prune properly; they are professionals. In order to protect your investment, and your personal safety, it may come down to money. Weedon says, "You wouldn't buy a great car and never wax it."

· 5 ·

Doors

What type of exterior doors provide the best security? Outside doors should be solid, with no windows, and they should be hinged to a good, strong frame. That is a great start, but there is far more to learn about doors. In our research, we found door sales people knew a lot about burglars. Why? Because one of the first things newly-burgled homeowners do is go to the door store. New doors, *and* frames, *and* better locks, are on the shopping lists. Door salespeople claim that *after* a crime a customer no longer quibbles about the high price of quality.

DOOR CONSTRUCTION

What should be of major concern for homeowners or renters is the type of exterior doors they have. Some doors are hollow. They were popular during the Forties, Fifties and Sixties. Hollow-core doors are light and cheap, filled with strips of wood or strips of paper. And there are a lot of spiral core doors around. They too are hollow and are filled with curls of wood, like the shavings you get when you plane a board. Spiral core doors are also light-weight. You can cut them with a boxknife. They usually hang on a house until a burglary occurs, or until a new owner wants them replaced with stronger doors. Check to see if you have one. If you do, replace it.

How do you know whether you have a hollow core door? Tap on it. It will sound like a drum—hollow. If you press on the face of the door, it will often move inward. Hollow core doors weigh around 30 pounds. Today's plain plywood doors of particle board, with sawdust and glue in the core, weigh about 90 pounds. They are as strong as any low-priced doors you can buy, according to door expert Ewell Fortner, who has been in the door business for forty years.

Fortner says the higher priced doors are usually better protection. That advice, of course, doesn't include design, which will be discussed later. "Higher priced doors usually have thicker inset panels," Fortner says, "and often have raised molding, which also gives added strength." Panels are anywhere from 7/16's of an inch to 3/8's of an inch thick. The thicker the panel, the better the door stands up to the sun and weather," Fortner said. "And the harder it will be to kick in." At a minimum, the width of your exterior door should be 1¾ inches.

Given a solid expensive door, the frame can be weak. Some, *not all*, developers have been hanging very impressive high-cost doors on cheap soft pine frames. Buyers examine the houses never realizing that secure, strong and very expensive doors are for looks alone; they won't keep intruders out. If a burglar or an enraged ex-boyfriend wants to come through, the door might stand the abuse. The frame won't. Get ready for company.

Some doors are made of metal and are filled with styrofoam. The styrofoam is injected under pressure and insulates well. This type of door is sold for its insulating quality, not for security.

Do you want a door no one can kick in? According to door experts, they haven't built one yet, not for the average home. Some up-scale buyers choose bank-vault doors and cover them with wood, but a homeowner has to be very afraid and very rich to try that solution. Drug dealers "rock houses" often have steel doors. You'd have to be a successful drug dealer to afford one.

Can you have glass in a door and still have security? That depends on the type of glass. You can buy triple glass—leaded glass in intricate, beautiful designs, sandwiched in between tempered safety glass. The air space inside makes a room quieter, it insulates and it is harder to break than regular glass. An added benefit—there is only one piece of glass to clean, even though the design may have one-hundred pieces in it. Wire mesh often is imbedded in glass, although its security value is debatable. It will not keep a burgler out.

"Burglar resistent" or "bullet-proof" glass in your front door may not keep bullets from an AK-47 out of your living

room. To be "burglar resistent," it must have many thick layers, according to "high-end" architects we interviewed. Of the
many wealthy clients who ask for it, few end up buying it. It is
too expensive.

How much can you expect to spend on a top-quality "high-
end" door? We saw one for nearly three-thousand dollars. It
was a single door, no frame. Most top-quality doors in urban
areas cost between fifteen-hundred to eighteen-hundred dollars, but a lot of that cost is for beauty and design. If you are
replacing doors in an existing home, those doors may cost even
more with the frames.

A strong door frame should be made of oak or teak. In a
large city, you can expect to pay around $375 for a doorframe
finished in teak. For solid oak, the cost-range is around $300.
Oak is the strongest wood used for door frames in the average-
priced home.

We must caution, no matter how strong your door and
doorframe, experienced burglars often by-pass front doors.
They will look for a raised foundation, crawl through a hole and
come up into a closet. Or, they will take shingles off the roof and
come into your home through the attic, thus the old police term,
"roof job." All you can do is "harden the target."

French Doors

The doors most likely to be penetrated are the popular and
very elegant French doors, comprised of nearly all glass, called
"lights," separated by thin frames. The divisions between the
"lights" can be built of weak or strong woods and enclose varied
thicknesses of glass. Depending upon design and price they can
be expensive. You can buy steel-framed French doors, although
they may have to be custom made. Steel frames can be textured
and painted to look like wood. They still will be elegant, but the
steel only solves the frame problem, not the problem of large,
vulnerable expanses of glass. The steel frame is useless, if one
window near the latch can be broken. The answer may be
triple-glass, but there are also security problems with its use.

The Problem with Triple Glass

Triple glass is usually 5/8 to 3/4 inches thick, which includes the dead air space inside. It is sealed as one solid unit,
although it still can be broken. According to door expert Ewell
Fortner, breaking the triple glass is like breaking a car wind-

shield. "You can hit it with a ten-pound block of wood, and it probably won't break," he said; "But with a pointed object, it's another story. It can shatter." Crooks know this. Be aware.

Fiberglass doors can be strong, *if* the fiberglass is thick and if the frame is also fiberglass or oak. Fiberglass doors can be very interesting looking, usually modern in design.

HINGES

Strong doors hung on strong frames can still be easily defeated *if* the door hinges are weak or incorrectly mounted. All door hinges, especially those on exterior doors, should be on the inside, *not* the outside, exposed to the sinister manipulation of burglars. All a burglar has to do, if he or she has a lot of time, is remove the screws holding the hinges to the frame, take off the hinges, and then remove the door. Presto—Entry. There are three easy ways to make sure this doesn't happen.

The first, and most logical way, is to simply remove the hinges and remount them on the inside of your home. This will make the door swing inward. A note: there are cities and states that prohibit doors from swinging inward. In an emergency, a number of people trying to exit in panic, "logjam," making it impossible to open the door. Check with your local fire marshal about such regulations. Define what your *own* concerns are.

The second way is to replace the screws holding the door hinges to the frame with "non-removable" screws. These screws have heads that only allow a screwdriver to move one way, the way it takes to screw them *into* wood. They cannot be unscrewed, and cannot be removed from the wood.

The last way is a little more difficult, takes more time, but works well. This method prevents a burglar from removing the hinges from your door. Take out the center (middle) screws from each door hinge on both sides (door and jamb), top and bottom. In the same places where you removed the screws (on the door side only), insert a bolt, nail, or "headless" screw. Make sure the bolts, nails, or screws you installed are sticking out of the hole about 1/2 inch. Now, when you shut the door, the bolt, nail, or "headless" screw you inserted on the door side will slide into the vacant hole opposite it on the jamb side. This forms two connections, top and bottom, between the door and the door frame. If a burglar removes the hinges and attempts to *life* the door, it will not move, for it is anchored to the door by the bolts, screws, or nails you installed. Tricky, but it works.

Glass Windows in Doors

If your door has a glass panel or glass decorative grill within forty-inches of the door lock, the lock is vulnerable to being unlocked by a burglar on the outside. The same is true of any glass within forty-inches of the lock, such as a window located near the door. This "forty-inch" rule is taken from the maximum length of a grown man's arm, extended through a broken or jimmied window, and reaching inside to unlock the inside door knob or dead-bolt latch.

If glass-work in your door, or a window within forty-inches of the door knob or door lock is not large enough to allow a man's arm to get through, then the odds against a break-in are diminished. Make sure that these openings or decorative spaces are no bigger than two-inches by two inches, or four-square-inches.

Sliding Glass Doors

Sliding glass doors are a security risk, but there are things you can do to diminish that risk. The best way to secure a sliding glass door is with a lock operated from the inside by a key. This lock should be sufficiently tight to remain engaged through any amount of movement or shaking. Supplemental locks should be installed at either the top or bottom of the glass door made of strong steel. These locks should be installed with the protruding bolts inserted at a slightly downward tilt.

Even some expensive sliding glass doors in multi-million dollar estates do not have adequate locking devices. It is possible, however, to secure these doors, even if the proper locks are not installed. The problem to overcome is they are not shatter-proof. All a burglar has to do is pick up a heavy object, and heave it through the sliding glass door. If the glass isn't safety glass, it's instant access. (Review the alarm chapter for alarms that detect breaking glass.) The vast majority of burglars want to get into your home undetected. Make it impossible for crooks to open your sliding glass door.

Place a dowel or slim broom-stick in the slider track of the glass doors, where the bottom of the steel frame slides back and forth. When the sliding glass door is shut, and the dowel is in place, the door cannot be opened by sliding it back; the presence of the dowel stops the door from moving. However, placing a dowel in the slider track will not completely protect the door from being defeated by a crook.

Most sliding glass doors have quite a bit of play between the top of the door and the frame. A grown man, with normal upper-body strength, can grip the glass door by the frame and outside handle and lift up, moving the door off its track and out of the frame. This can be prevented by making certain the door and frame are tight together. It is simple to do.

Since the slider frame is installed into the home's walls *before* the glass door is mounted by lifting it in, the glass door can be lifted out of the frame. Lift the glass door out and set it aside. In the upper, horizontal door frame, at the center and on both ends, insert several #8 or #10, or 1¼-inch pan-head (large head) sheet-metal screws. Adjust these screws so that the top of the door is flush against them, after it has been replaced in the slider frame. The space between the top of the glass door and the bottom of the upper frame has been eliminated. The sliding glass door now cannot be lifted out of the frame.

Security Screen Doors

As discussed in other chapters, it is preferable to layer a home's defenses so that a burglar or determined intruder is forced to overcome many obstacles, not just one, to gain entry into your house. A good barrier is the security screen door, not to be confused with the standard screen door.

The security screen door is made of tough, tempered steel mesh or wire that is cut-resistant. These doors have solid steel frames and can be locked. Some security screen doors have two layers of screening, one wide-mesh to deter criminals, and the other a smaller mesh, primarily to screen against insects. Hinges on a screen door are reversed and capped. The purpose of the security screen door is to prevent tampering of the primary exterior door.

It is important that a door does not have too much play between it and the frame, or the door jamb. If it does, it will be possible for an intruder to use a pry-bar or stout knife to pry his way inside. Examine doors of older homes carefully to see if the structure of entry has shrunk away from its support. This examination should include the doorstop, which prevents the door from swinging the wrong way. If you find weaknesses, too much space, which would allow a strong knife to penetrate, you may need to have someone reinforce the door. However, a strong deadbolt lock, with at least a one-inch throw, *should* "hold" your door.

6

Weapons, Yours
and Theirs

Few crooks carry only one weapon. They usually have back-up weapons hidden from view, either on them or within reach. Several years ago, one of the most successful advertising campaigns for Bianchi International, a maker of police holsters, showed John Bianchi, the CEO of the company, in a tuxedo. The slogan above him read, "Wolf in Sheep's Clothing." An inset at the bottom of the ad, with Bianchi in his underwear, revealed he was wearing 27 concealed handguns beneath the tuxedo. Not one of the weapons showed. If you attempt to gain the advantage with a suspect, and if you win, your advantage may be only temporary. In such circumstances, police are ready for surprises. Most citizens are not and haven't a clue as to what to expect.

If you are in a stand-off with a crook, do not forget that he or she may have two, three or more concealed weapons of various descriptions, weapons like you have never seen before. What is frightening is many won't look like weapons at all.

Criminals can shave down a credit card until it is as sharp as a knife. Some gangmembers wear a small unobtrusive spike that protrudes from their shoelaces. The spikes can be hard to spot, under the inner-city fashions of baggy pants. One surprise kick in an especially vulnerable place, and you are his victim.

Don't think a "Blood" or a "Crip" can't be in your neighborhood. "Bloodbath" Jones may have been kicked out of the house in Compton, California, and he's moved to your town to live with his grandmother. Or, the heat is on in L. A. because of a crime he's committed there, and he's slipped out of town for awhile to vacation in Little Rock with Aunt Marge. According to the Los Angeles gang tracking system, gangmembers are in all fifty states dealing drugs. Their weapons are often unusual and deadly. Get used to it. Look for more than a gun or a knife.

An imported trick from south of the border is for a crook to spit in your face. When you wipe away the spittle, you slice your own cheek from the sliver of razorblade he carries in his mouth for just such emergencies. While you are perplexed, he takes the advantage.

Crooks are not as caring as they once were. The honor code of the old crime families is all but gone. Today's criminals *will* hurt women and children. In West Coast home invasions, babies have been tortured in front of parents because residents wouldn't reveal where valuables were hidden. Do the home invasions happen only on the West Coast? No. West Coast invaders have been known to drive or fly thousands of miles to do their work. In today's criminal world, anything goes . . . and often does. *No* "ordinary" citizen can be prepared for the criminals that exist today.

No problem, you say? You were a ranger in Vietnam and can handle yourself against an armed and determined enemy? Think again, bucko, for a lot of police officers in Los Angeles and other big cities were rangers, special forces, recon marines, and other elites in the late, great Republic of Vietnam . . . and they *still* get taken on the street by crooks. For instance, don't copy what you see on television. Police officers, as a general rule, think cop shows on TV are stupid, written by writers who don't have a clue about what real crooks are like.

Let's say you, the concerned citizen, want to put your crook into a wall search position until the real police officers get there? Most West Coast police officers know that the wall search position, the traditional "grab the wall" posture taken by criminals to be searched, can be a trap. Bad guys in "crook school"—any state prison—learn to drop to their knees while in the wall search position, entangle the searching officer's feet and pull him or her off balance. They then take the officer's weapon and make the kill.

Another ploy used by street crooks and gangsters is to grab the top of a Beretta 92F handgun, or "Police Special," while covered. A quick scuffle ensues and the victim triumphantly retrieves the Beretta and immediately covers the crook again, this time warily making sure the weapon is out of arm's reach.

No problem, you say? The problem is that the crook disconnected the slide mechanism of the Beretta during that brief struggle. Now the firearm cannot be fired. It's worthless. The slide to the Beretta? It's in the assailant's hand. It could happen to you. And you will be *real* lucky, if after this confrontation, your assailant is running away from you. It pays to know your enemy and know what *he* knows.

SHOULD YOU OWN
A HANDGUN?

Much has been written about owning firearms. We will deal briefly with both sides of that issue. First, a statement by a representative of the National Rifle Association, the NRA:

Tracy Martin, a certified National Rifle Association instructor, states that the NRA, which has been very militant about preventing waiting periods for handgun ownership and even regulation of military assault weapons ownership, was formed to "promote civilian marksmanship to protect the Constitution." Ms. Martin also said the NRA "promotes hunting as a viable method for controlling wildlife resources." Over the assault weapon controversy and waiting period legislation, particularly the Brady Bill, police leadership and the National Rifle Association have split ranks in recent years.

According to Ms. Martin, the current NRA position on handgun ownership for self-protection is not whether a homeowner *should* have a gun but that they have a *right* to own a gun. "We encourage people who buy firearms to get the proper training," she said. "Many things can go wrong if you do not have proper training." (More information about classes is available through the NRA Headquarters in Washington D.C. Telephone: 1-800-368-5714.) You do not have to be a member of the National Rifle Association to take part in their gun-safety classes.

Should Guns Be Kept in the
Home for Self-Protection?

Sarah Brady of Handgun Control Inc. and the Washington D.C. Center to Prevent Handgun Violence wrote the following essay for *Home Safe Home*.

The increase in violent crime in America has caused most Americans to give greater thought to their personal safety.

As more and more people do this, many consider purchasing a firearm for self-protection. This decision, however, cannot be made without first learning the facts.

Most law enforcement officers do not recommend firearms as a means of self-protection. "If guns were the answer to the threat of violent crime, we'd sell them at police stations," said Baltimore County Police Chief Neil Behan. Police safety experts recommend increased lighting, alarm systems and neighborhood watch programs. In addition, a survey by Figgie International found that imprisoned armed robbers would protect their own homes with dogs rather than guns. (Author's note: ex-felons may not legally carry guns.)

Those concerned with their safety should consider a form of protection which cannot be turned against them. In 1989, 25 percent of the law enforcement officers killed with handguns in the line of duty *were killed with their own handguns.*

The very existence of a firearm in the home presents increased risk to the family it is supposed to protect. 1,500 Americans are killed accidentally with firearms annually, one-third of whom are children. In fact, one child a day is killed in a handgun accident.

Guns in the home also offer an easy means of suicide. The odds that a suicidal teen will commit suicide go up 75 percent when a gun is kept in the home.

A study published in *The New England Journal of Medicine* in 1986 found that for every instance when a family handgun was used to kill an intruder, 43 family members, friends and acquaintances died. "The advisability of keeping firearms in the home for protection must be questioned," the study concluded. The decision to bring a handgun in the home should be made responsibly after considering all the facts and understanding the risks involved. It should never be made out of fear or in a panic situation. The results can be deadly. (By Sarah Brady of Handgun Control Inc., and the Washington D.C. Center to Prevent Handgun Violence.)

The International Association of Chiefs of Police (IACP) is the world's most prestigious and powerful association of police executives, with over 12,500 members from 73 different nations. As a body, its members are the most educated and highly trained police administrators, in comparison to members of newer, smaller, regional police associations.

IACP's position on firearms management is parallel with its support for the right of law-abiding Americans to have firearms for legitimate sporting and recreational, law enforcement, and private security uses. The IACP *does not believe*, however, that the right to bear arms guaranteed by the Second Amendment to the United States Constitution implies or compels the unfettered proliferation of firearms among citizens. "Indeed, prudence, common sense, and wisdom dictate otherwise," states their media release to HOME SAFE HOME. The paper continues:

"Unfortunately, crime is only part of the total problem with guns. Consider for a moment that every year there are over one million "gun incidents" in the United States. This includes nearly 11,000 murders involving firearms, 15,000 suicides, 1,900 accidental deaths, 175,200 criminal assaults committed with firearms, 221,000 armed robberies, 90,400 forcible rapes, and over 200,000 gun-related injuries. All told, an estimated 130 million firearms exist in America today. That is one for every two households. Nearly 70 million of these firearms are handguns, the type used in three-fourths of all the gun incidents. Nearly 5.5 million firearms are manufactured and 750,000 more are imported each year. Unlike products that wear out, guns last almost indefinitely and actually increase in value. Each year in the state of Florida alone, over 350,000 guns are assembled from imported parts and sold for less than $100 each. Almost all the weapons manufactured are sold initially by over 200,000 firearms dealers, some of whom operate gun shops, but many others sell weapons in service stations and country stores. Most gun dealers are individuals who get the ten-dollar federal license to qualify for discounts and mail purchases. Gun thefts from manufacturers, dealers, and private citizens now exceed one-half million annually. Weapons acquired for self-defense by private citizens are prime targets for thieves and often are stolen because of infrequent security measures."

THE OTHER SIDE

Some citizens who have already become victims argue that things have gone too far; that it is now necessary for honest citizens to have handguns for protection, especially in America's cities, because police are so under-resourced and criminals have become so unfeeling. Sharon McComb, a former Sixties activist who requested government placement in Watts after the 1965 riots, and who was a gun-control proponent for years, says she evolved into a gun-owner within the last two years. "When I finally bought my Baretta in the summer of 1992, I found it difficult to even touch it," she said. "It made my skin crawl. But with the savagery of the crimes in my city, and the sociopathic behavior I read about, I now find it a necessity. If I need help, I am no longer confident police can arrive in time, or under some circumstances, that they will be able to arrive at all."

Gun Dealers

Do statistics uphold IACP philosophy *and* the fears of law-abiding citizens? In Los Angeles in 1991, 8,000 people were treated for gunshot wounds in the city's hospitals. That is far more than the number of Americans killed during the Persian Gulf War. According to police, there are more shootings than those recorded. Criminals who are on parole, or who have outstanding warrants, will not go to an emergency room unless their lives are in danger. "Kitchen nurses" take care of the wounds. These are victims uncounted.

Statistics on gun sales and victimization are beginning to be a bore. You've probably heard it all before, but the numbers are getting staggering. Let us examine one city: In 1991, one in six Los Angeles households were victimized by crimes where handguns were used. Of 1,100 federally licensed gun dealers in Los Angeles County, fewer than 150 registered or even bought permits. Gun dealers operate out of homes, out of their cars, and on the streets. It is estimated that over 3,000 gun dealers actually operate in L.A. The U.S. Treasury Department's Bureau of Alcohol, Tobacco and Firearms is sorely under-funded. The ability of the Bureau to keep up with illegal gun sales is termed, by many police experts, as impossible. There is no "daylight" on this issue.

7

You Still Feel
Compelled to Buy
a Gun?

How do the police experts feel about firearms in the hands of citizens? Los Angeles County Sheriff's detective, Steve Rubino, says, "If you buy a handgun, make sure you learn how to use it. Go to a class. You *have* to watch out for the kids. You'll hear people advise that you should keep the gun in one place, and the ammunition in another. A handgun is not to scare someone. If you have to use it, it's no good if it's unloaded! You have to pick a safe storage spot. Teach the kids *never* to touch it. Lock it up somewhere. For a woman, I'd choose a .380. (Many handguns, because of their weight, their size and the strength it takes to pull the trigger, are cumbersome for a woman's smaller hands.) A Walther PPKS is not difficult to handle. They make fairly small nine-millimeters, perfect for women. Have a few extra boxes of ammunition, and a few extra magazines."

(Note: *The Safety Zone*, Telephone: 800-999-3030, has a mail-order lockbox to prevent handgun accidents. It is a quick-action small safe, advertised as difficult for smaller children to get into. It bolts to the bottom of a drawer, and has a pre-set programmable combination.)

A caution: Los Angeles today is like the "Wild, Wild West." Rubino's words must be taken in the context of where he does his police work, what he has seen on the streets, and the fact that he works career criminals *only*. Boston's Sergeant Richard Doyle, although he also has seen the worst of crimes, does not approve of weapons in the home *at all*. Doyle recalled a young woman in a basement apartment who shot and killed her rapist. "But for every one of those, there are twenty others where a victim's gun was turned against him," he says. "Having a weapon in the house gives the intruder one more thing to use against you." Does Doyle have guns in his own home? Yes. All police officers own guns. "But in my neighborhood," he says, "I'm going to be the first guy who gets 'whacked.' God forbid a police officer responds, and the burglar in my house has a loaded gun."

WILL YOUR GUN GET INTO
HANDS OF CRIMINALS?

Chief of Police George Colgin of Fort Scott, Kansas, voiced his frustrations with the problems police have with stolen guns, even in his small town of 8,400 inhabitants. *Handguns travel.* "We don't get many recoveries of stolen guns," Colgin says. "What we're finding out, is these things are being traced down the line to other 'druggies.' Here, they *aren't* being fenced."

The weapon *you* own may one day be used in a crime. It is sought-after "booty" by burglars. It will "fence" easily. It is a stirring note that the handgun that killed Bobby Kennedy was purchased by a homeowner for self-protection after the Watts Riots in 1965.

According to FBI statistics, firearms are used in three of every five murders committed in the United States. Of those murders for which weapons were reported, 50 percent were by handguns, 6 percent by shotguns, and 4 percent by rifles. Unknown types of firearms accounted for the other percent.

WHEN YOU INSIST ON
HAVING A WEAPON, BUT
YOU DON'T WANT A GUN

DYEWitness Criminal Identifier. As protection against assaults, DYEWitness, fights back with a 70 lb. blast of foaming green dye. It must be used at close range, safely within five-and-half feet. Stinging upon contact, it foams over the attacker's face. It obscures vision, *if* you are a good aim. Totally dispensed, which takes seven seconds, DYEWitness leaves a green stain on the attacker's face for up to seven days, making it easier for police identification. Manufactured in Mississauga, Ontario, Canada.

CAP-STUN. CAP-STUN is oleoresin capsicum at 5.5 strength cayenne pepper base solution with cosmetic alcohol base. It is dispersed in mist form. Often referred to as O/C, CAP-STUN comes in mace-sized containers and is issued by the FBI to its agents. This product is sold through the mail, and in many states CAP-STUN is sold over the counter. CAP-STUN and MACE are very different. CAP-STUN affects four major areas: the eyes, the respiratory system, the skin and muscle coordination. After a one-second burst, a person's eyes will not stay open, it takes ten to thirty minutes for full function of the airways to return to normal, and the skin will feel like it's on fire. The pain is far worse than MACE. Exposure may cause a person to lose balance. The average distance for firing CAP-STUN is 10 to 15 feet. One law enforcement bulletin stated: "CAP-STUN will make you feel like you are going to die." This is a product that we feel should be regulated, and should definitely not be sold through the mail.

STUN GUN. The stun gun is an electronic device which typically puts out 120,000 volts of current from two 9-volt batteries. The stun gun comes in different forms: a baton—a seven-inch by two-and-one-half inch device; and a small pocket zapper the size of a beeper which puts out 50,000 volts. Manufacturers advertise that the mere sight of a stun gun will intimidate most attackers. That is true, unless the attacker is incredibly stupid or is under the influence of drugs. *Many* are.

A stun gun overpowers nerve impulses to muscles. It removes voluntary muscle control causing mental confusion. A stun gun does *not* affect nerve impulses going to the heart and other involuntary organs; however, the experience of being "stunned" can cause a heart attack.

After using a stun gun, it is prudent to retain contact with the assailant for five seconds, even as the person is falling to the ground. Stun guns cause severe pain on a person not under the influence of drugs or large amounts of alcohol. When using the stun gun, the metal probes must actually touch the body of your assailant. The shock can be felt through heavy clothing. The degree of the shock depends on the size of the assailant, how long contact is made, and where contact is made. It is best to make contact with the stomach, below the rib cage and the sides, especially the underarm area; but don't risk yourself trying to touch that especially sensitive target.

Stun guns are advertised as working efficiently within twenty-feet of an assailant. You must call your local police agency to determine whether a stun gun is legal in your area. Most stun guns cost between 60 to 150 dollars. Stun guns may be purchased by mail-order or through police and security products stores.

Kiyoga Steel Whip and Spiro. The Kiyoga is a steel whip about 17-inches long. It extends, and when closed is about the size of a cigar. It is comfortably carried in a purse. A flick of the wrist extends the weapon. You should check your local police department to find out if possession of this weapon violates any concealed weapon law. Remember, anyone can have a weapon taken away and used against them. Also, in today's litigious environment, you can be sued for using *any* weapon on *anyone*.

The Spiro also can be carried in a purse or pocket. The Spiro is not *supposed* to fracture bones or break the flesh. It stings. It also can put out an eye. A lot of freaky things can happen when an untrained person uses an exotic weapon. The Spiro and the Kiyoga Steel Whip cost between 30 and 60 dollars. We don't recommend them.

Prosecutor-24 (PR-24) Side-Handle Baton. Rated by police as far superior to ordinary police batons and a weapon that makes police defense attorneys weep, it is sold to the public in most states. The PR-24 has 4 to 9 times the striking power of the old "hickory" style of baton and can do a lot of tissue damage. It also can be used for fence climbing, armlocks, and take-downs, *if* you know what you are doing. Police take classes to learn how to use it. The PR-24 is 24-inches long and is constructed of steel-strength plastic. It is available in most security industry and police uniform and equipment stores at a cost of about twenty-five or thirty dollars. It is also sold by The Spy Factory, headquartered in San Antonio, Texas. You must check with your local police department to learn if ownership of this weapon violates the law. We do not recommend the PR-24 for use by anyone other than a police professional, well-trained in its use. A police professional, on the average, takes twenty-four hours of initial instruction on its use. Instructors are usually personnel from the Manadnock Lifetime Products Company.

8

Security "Experts"
and Consultants

Be very cautious when you see the words "experts" and "consultants." The terms "expert" and "consultant" are not inter-changeable, since not all experts are consultants, and not all consultants are experts. Specialties include executive protection (physical protection of dignitaries and security plans for them and their families), physical security (security of buildings and grounds), personal protection (includes body guards), computer and information security, and others. The "experts" and "consultants" advertise in the yellow pages of your telephone directory, in classified ads in your newspapers, and through local associations and organizations. Security consulting is a booming business, and it is getting bigger.

In many states, security consulting requires no licensing or government monitoring. Some states provide conduct standards for security guard agencies, for private investigators, alarm installers, monitoring stations, and for automobile repossessors. But, for security consultants? They often fall into a grey area that is not policed.

Most security consultants try to give customers their money's worth. It is a way of making a business grow, but consulting is still a business, not a public entity. The consultant is not required "to do the right thing." A consultant who provides shoddy service, or whose services are overpriced, will eventually fail. That doesn't help the customers' hurt during the early part of his or her time on the streets.

Most security consultants are former police officers (especially police managers), federal agents of some sort, or retired military law enforcement officers. There are capable consulting firms operating in larger cities today, headed by retired or former FBI Special Agents, military intelligence officers, and retired civilian police managers.

Most major companies that deal with executive protection, not including the standard "bodyguard" mill of large urban areas, are headed by former or retired Secret Service Special Agents. Since personal protection was their government stock and trade, most of them make reasonably good consultants in this field.

The more successful investigative consultant will have many years of experience as a detective with a large police agency, as a federal criminal investigator, or many, many years as a major corporate investigator. In this arena, the retired or former military investigator, with no civilian experience, is not considered as skilled at convoluted investigations requiring in-depth knowledge of contemporary investigative techniques. However, the consulting field of physical security is heavy with retired military personnel developing their second career.

The providing of bodyguards is usually limited to retired or off-duty police officers who retain their legal ability to carry concealed firearms, since most people fearful for their safety would not hire an unarmed bodyguard. On rare occasions, an unarmed bodyguard will be approved by a client, due to the protector's larger physical size, intimidating appearance, demeanor, or skill in unarmed combat or martial arts, or the client's special physical demand.

How Do You Choose a Reputable Consultant?

1. First, ask you local police department's Community Services Officer or Public Relations Officer if the state, county or city licenses and/or regulates the security business, and in particular, the security consulting business. If a license or board examination is required, the first question you ask is "Do you have a license?" Don't take their word for it. Ask to see the license, or go to the business and look for the license. Photocopies can be altered. Don't trust a photocopy. Call the licensing office and check on the license.

2. Ask for references of satisfied clients. In some cases, customers will not want that information shared. They may not want it on record that they had need of a security consultant. In this event, ask for corporate or organizational references: boating clubs, civic associations, businesses. A reputable consultant will be eager to share this information.

3. Verify the consultant's professional history. Request his or her biography, a written document that lists job titles, security or police experience, academic credentials, memberships, and other accomplishments in the field of security. Pay close attention to how long the consultant has been in business. Was he a "career hopper?" An interesting note on a security consultant we know is that he lists jobs he held while in prison. There is no mention in the documents that he *was* in prison, although the expertise he learned there is of tremendous value to his clients. He hides nothing. After his initial introduction, he shows clippings about his trial and the controversy surrounding his case. Then he gets down to the mean business of crime and criminals and how to stop them.

4. Look for verifiable means of competency. Has the consultant published articles for journals or newspapers? Is he a consultant for major national organizations, for conventions, for a business concern involved in the Olympics? Has he or she published a book? If a book is listed, ask to see a copy for review. There are some vanity press publications being advertised on this subject, with dubious, high-minded sounding qualifications of the writers. In one newspaper series sent to us, a retired military officer selling his seminars as an "expert in executive protection" left out the rudiments in window and door security. The danger was great, for he miseducated the population of that newspapers' circulation. Following his instructions, which were tragically incomplete, residents were lulled into a false sense of security. After all, he was an "expert." The newspaper printed his supposed knowledge, gained in a "fly-by-night" class taught by other "fly-by-night" instructors. *Real* security consultants and police officers lucky enough to be in law enforcement agencies that offer up-to-date and *very* expensive training, call them "the wanna-be's." The "wanna-be's" can do a lot of damage. Be cautious.

It helps to authenticate a consultant's education level. His or her knowledge of diverse subjects, always an asset for a security consultant, should be strong if the consultant has a four-year degree, at minimum. Sometimes, the absence of an *accredited* college degree means the difference between *good* and *outstanding* service. Another caution: If you don't know much about college and university degrees, you can call your reference librarian at your local library and check out the validity of the school's degree.

5. For added insurance, check with the local Better Business Bureau and the Chamber of Commerce about your consultant's business practices. Keep in mind that these services will keep only *written* complaints on file for protection against civil suits lodged by business people who may find complaints unfounded or petty.

6. Check with your consultant's competitors. Keep in mind, no one wants to give away business. Most business people understand that talking badly about a competitor, without good reason, will boomerang and hurt future business projects. Most competitors will give an honest opinion, however, "veiled" from their exposure to the consultant in business dealings, participation in civic organizations, or social and religious activities. Get several opinions. Do not rely on the words of only one person. Take excessive applause or excessive castigation with caution.

· 9 ·

The Difference
Between "Police"
and "Security"

Police and security work are often world's apart in the skills and knowledge each requires. A good police officer may never be a competent security consultant, yet he is taken as such by the average citizen and even the corporate CEO. When it comes to the more sophisticated security work, people often associate the uniforms, badges and guns of both occupations. That is a mistake. Police enforce public laws, with all the majesty of the governing body they represent. Security operatives protect private property and "private" persons. Security operatives have more limited power than do police, and legally, either in or out of uniform, they remain "private" citizens.

While most police patrol officers and police managers are knowledgable about laws, the courts, local crooks and criminal behavior, they are most often critically short on security knowledge. This expertise includes lighting, barriers and how they can be used, locks and locking devices, computer security issues, access control (especially automated access control), alarm systems and approved monitoring stations, private personnel screening techniques, and sophisticated audio and video monitoring electronics. Most police officers entering the security field find that the majority of the knowledge they learned in law enforcement is virtually worthless; most retired police executives, on the other hand, are usually hired into private security for their business expertise, personal contacts within the business community and their mature administrative demeanor, which is great for a security company's image. They are *not* hired for their in-depth knowledge of private security policies and procedures or ever-changing equipment. It is important that a security consultant not rely on his or her reputation as "a great cop." You must remember that, as well. If you want a police officer, call one. If you need a security consultant, find "a great cop" who has years of experience in his or her *new* profession.

HOW MUCH SHOULD YOU PAY?

Fees for security consulting vary widely, depending upon whether the consultant is working for a corporation or for an individual homeowner. Also dependent is what the background of the consultant is and how valued is his knowledge. As in other businesses, a lot rests on supply and demand. A personal protection consultant may charge fifty dollars an hour in Salt Lake City, Utah, and two-hundred dollars an hour in Chicago. Just as you would shop around for a car, compare and shop for a security consultant. Find out what the going rate is in the major cities in your state. You can contact the American Society of Industrial Security in Washington, D.C., for names of certified consultants in your area. Don't forget, you usually get what you pay for.

When do you pay the consultant? Unless you pay a small retainer fee, do not pay for the services until the work has been done. Ask for a formal billing. Should you insist upon a formal contract? Yes. Have a lawyer or a paralegal examine the contract if you feel you don't have the skills to do so yourself. Ensure the following items are covered:

EXACTLY what services are to be performed? Inspection of premises and recommendation of security devices? Installation of alarms (audible or silent)? Testing of these alarms? Installation of window grills (breakaway or secured)? Installation of upgraded security lighting? Upgraded locks? Obtaining of a personal duress notification system?

EXACTLY when and where will these services take place? The contract must state that the consultant will make one or more visual inspection of your residence, making written recommendations about security needs, provide a written estimate of cost, list where the services may be obtained, and when (or under what circumstances) the contract will be considered fully executed.

EXACTLY how much you are going to pay the consultant, and what are the terms of that payment? The amount may be stated as a fixed fee, a percentage of the cost of the upgrades, or an amount to be paid to the consultant by the week or month. Beware of fee percentages. An unscrupulous consultant may take the opportunity to inflate his or her income by recommending excessively high-priced hardware and also may pump up the installation costs. The fee schedule in the contract should be simple and easy to understand.

The fee schedule should elaborate upon each service the consultant is to perform: premises inspection, travel expenses (if any), report and schematic preparation, and any other out-of-pocket expenses. Make sure the contract states that your payment is not due until the consultant provides you with the written report, including what he or she did, what is recommended, and a cost estimate of each implementation of the recommendations.

Make sure the consultant will submit a written report of how you are to enhance your security and the security of your family, risks from people or animals, security risks from the elements, security risks from the residence structure itself, and what hardware or behavior changes are recommended to defeat forced entry into your home.

Remember, security consultants are like everything else—there are good ones and bad ones, expensive ones and cheap ones, talented ones and incompetent ones. Shop around.

Locks and Locksmiths

"Locks are for honest people" Boston Police Sergeant Richard Doyle told us. To "professional" thieves and burglars, they are little more than a nuisance. Yet today, few people would leave their homes or apartments without locking doors and windows. Good locks deter amateur thieves and thwart the "pro's" who are looking for an easy "hit."

Some locks are so ineffective it makes no difference whether they are locked or not. Even amateur criminals will get through some of them. "Hardening the target" means that any lock is better than no lock at all. For the seasoned burglar or a determined rapist who has chosen his victim, or the sweating "druggie" desperately in need of "coke" money, the determination to get into your home renders most locks, even the more sophisticated ones, ineffective. It is easy to break a window. Security is never an absolute.

THE TECHNICAL ASPECTS
OF LOCKS

One of the most ineffective locks today is the near-ancient "warded lock." In the simplest of terms, it is a mechanical lock, one that was first developed centuries ago and operates with a skeleton key. It works by use of a key designed to miss certain obstacles inside the lock, called "wards," thus triggering the release of a stout spring which pulls the bolt back from the door jamb. It's greatest weakness is its vulnerability to manipulation of its interior spring by any key that can move the old interior wards. Even unskilled crooks can rotate the lock action and drive or withdraw the bolt with a crude, improvised key, even a bent metal coat-hanger. If you vacation in those fancy old inns filled with antiques, you may still find warded locks and skeleton keys. No one serious about security would use a warded lock. Insist upon their replacement wherever they are found.

A second, almost "useless lock," is the door chain. They are ridiculously weak, and present virtually no obstacle to strong force. Don't depend on one for safety. Talk *through* the closed door to strangers. Install a peephole.

Markedly improved, and far harder to open without the proper key, is the "lever lock." In the lever lock, a number of lever tumblers are retained in a certain position by a strong spring. Each lever is designed to accomodate a lug, which is linked to the bolt. This is called a "fence," and it must slide into the cuts on the levers, for the bolt to be withdrawn. Nearly all mechanical locks today are variations of the lever lock. If it sounds complicated, you'll understand why the lever lock is vastly superior to the warded lock. A good locksmith could write paragraphs and talk for hours about the operation of the lever lock. What is important to the consumer is that it's a giant step up from the warded lock, and it can use two keys. If an apartment manager or homeowner wants the use of a special master key, lever locks can be "master-keyed." Even though the lever lock can be picked or "manipulated," it takes someone with special lock-pick tools, training, and experience—a "pro." The problem is, there are a lot of pro's out there.

With the "pin tumbler lock," it is necessary to use a key to both open and close the lock. A disadvantage to this lock is that if it has been "master-keyed," it is easier for a crook to pick it. The advantage of this lock is obvious, since if a burglar who entered your home by the window wanted to take your television, VCR, or other bulky items out the front door (which was locked with a pin tumbler lock), he would have a very difficult time. All big items, stereos, microwave ovens, heavy tool boxes, will be harder to steal. The disadvantage to you, the resident, is that you need to have keys in handy, hard-to-find places, especially at night, in case there is a fire and you have to exit your home quickly. However, in the words of master locksmith Tom Vessels, who has dealt with locks, keys, and safes for over thirty years, "If there's a fire, you can pick up something heavy and break a window. You wouldn't burn yourself up, because you didn't want to break a window. You have to figure out what makes you feel insecure the most, and take care of that."

It is possible to change or rearrange tumblers within a lock, if you want to change a key or several keys. These changes can be done time and time again. This is practical if you live in a large home and have a succession of many guests, several of them at one time, or an unending string of new wives or husbands, and dependent children. You would naturally be concerned, just as a hotel manager would be, that someone could return later with their room key and pilfer your property, or the property of the newest guest in the room. However, if you live in a huge home with many, many guest rooms, you may not want to use one master key plan. If that master key gets out, or is lost, your entire security system is compromised. Use one, two, even three master key plans, depending upon the size of your estate. Divide the estate into access areas, such as a series or number of bedrooms in one area, stables and garage in another area, and so on. A series of master key set-ups will greatly enhance security.

The only problem in changing tumblers within a lock is if your locks have been "master-keyed." You will have to preserve the old key signature system in each lock that allows a master-key to open it. Also, through rearranging the inside of each lock, it is possible to take a lock *out* of a master key plan for additional security. Unless you are a genuine inventor, tinkerer, or certified locksmith, changing tumblers, epsecially with a master-key system, should be left to others more qualified.

Electromechanical locks work with a combination of electrical and mechanical functions. Generally, a mechanical latch is either inserted into or withdrawn from a striker plate when electricity is applied to the mechanism. Usually, a solenoid is the engine that delivers a magnetic pull or push to the bolt, or releases a latch keeper. Electromagnetic locks have been used for years in business offices, apartment houses, condominiums, and commercial buildings. Generally, the electromagnet inside the locking device is energized at all times, keeping the magnet activated against the door striker, keeping the door closed and locked. When the flow of electricity is stopped, the magnet ceases to function and the door unlocks and opens.

The electromagnetic lock works similarly to the electromechanical lock, but has no mechanical parts. This lock is merely an electrical magnet that, when receiving electricity, sticks to a metal striker plate and keeps the door from moving. Normally, there are several magnets arrayed along the door line, each exerting a strong magnetic force against adjoining striker plates. Up to 1,500 pounds of force can be exerted in this way, making for an effective door lock. This lock is so effective that, in the event the door is attacked by force, such as with a sledgehammer or drill, other parts of the door and door-frame will be defeated before the electromagnetic lock will fail. However, it is dependent upon an outside power source—electricity. If you cannot afford a back-up generator to ensure continued energy to the lock, maybe this devise is not for you.

Electronic locks incorporate some sort of logic control to either a mechanical or electromechanical lock. This logic control takes the form of a required digital sequence applied on a key pad before the lock can be opened, and in some cases, closed. We've all seen this type of lock, or logic control device. It resembles a digital telephone, with numbers from 1 to 9, and a zero. Anyone desiring to enter a room or space controlled by an electronic lock simply enters his or her code (required digital sequence) by pressing the numbered buttons. Some electronic locks require a coded identification card to be inserted into a slot, accompanied by a personal code punched into the key pad, before the logic control signals the lock to work. If the code is correct, the logic control allows electricity to pass from the power source to the lock, which then either inserts or retracts a deadbolt.

A problem with electronic locks and some logic controls is that they can be easily fooled. A Los Angeles engineer refashioned an access card of his estranged wife, making a replica card that included the small, encased magnets that contain information which allows access. It was a relatively easy thing for him to do. He was able to enter her parking garage, and later her apartment, to investigate her new life. An entry system that requires more than a card for access, one that requires an accompanying personal identification code, adds a superior dimension of security.

Some electonic locks have devices that identify false-starts and incorrect code entries. After a certain number of incorrect combinations of numbers have been entered, the logic device either shuts down or notifies the authorities that an attempt has been made to subvert the system. In some sophisticated systems, the electronic lock key-pad is located in a room which can be secured or locked by command from the electronic lock. If a series of incorrect codes is entered into the data pad, the logic device shuts down, notifies security personnel, and the door locks activate, trapping the person who entered the false data. When security personnel arrive at the "man-trap," the suspect is still waiting, a prisoner.

The final type of lock that we occasionally see and operate is the dial-type combination lock. Even though these locks do not use a key, they still operate on the same principle as lever tumbler locks; they operate by aligning tumbler gates to allow insertion of the fence on the bolt. By manipulating the dial on the front of the door, usually a safe, the tumblers inside are moved to align the interior gates, in sequence, according to a combination of numbers. When all the numbers have been aligned, the fence falls and the bolt retracts. Normally, the combination is completed and then a lever must be pulled to physically retract the bolt or bolts from the striker plates. A common practice of people who operate dial-type combination locks each day is to manipulate the dial up to the last number of the combination, usually a zero, and leave it that way at the end of the day. The idea is, that the following morning all they have to do is move the dial to the zero, either left or right, and the lever can be pulled, retracting the bolts and opening the safe. They don't have to go to all the trouble of going through the combination again.

The problem here is that a skilled burglar, knowing of this common practice, will simply move the dial, deliberately and slowly, until the last gate is aligned and the fence falls into place. He has moved the dial to zero, just like the unsuspecting employee had planned to do on the following morning. Except, the smart burglar did it the night before.

A LOCK EXPERT SHARES
WHAT HE KNOWS

Our lock expert, Tom Vessels, operates a lock service in a major metropolitan area. His address and the city where he operates will not be shared because the most highly skilled locksmiths can be threatened with kidnap and injury for use of their expertise.

Vessels has been in the business for over thirty years. His father was a locksmith, before him. That's where he learned the craft, from sweeping floors in his father's shop to managing a large, thriving enterprise with many certified employees. He's also a state-certified contractor and is licensed to open, sell, repair, and install locks.

He first discussed deadbolt locks. It had been suggested to us by a police executive in the Midwest that homeowners only buy locks with throws (bolts) one-and-a-half inches long, and that the standard one-inch deadbolt was no longer satisfactory. "There is only one company manufacturing them," Vessels said. "It's Armstrong. And an inch-and-a-half isn't going to do that much better."

Vessels says that the trick to making a good deadbolt work is not the added half-inch but the quality of the throw (the extended bolt), the locking device, *and* the strike (the part where the bolt enters on the door jamb).

"I torture test new products when they come out," Vessels says. "I beat them up. With hammers, crowbars. We pick them, which is fairly easy for a locksmith, a professional."

Locks for Bedrooms

People who feel especially vulnerable, such as those who already have been victimized or who have received threats of physical harm, should have pin tumbler locks installed on the master bedroom doors. Perfect for people who live alone, this provides another barrier through which a burglar or rapist must pass, thus delaying him long enough for the resident to summon the police. (If you have children in your home, this arrangement may not be for you. *Definitely*, this lock suggestion should not be used in a child's room.)

Although burglary is a crime of stealth, rape is not. Women have been raped inside their homes, in their own bedrooms, after their husbands were murdered. Sexist or not, it is a fact that women are usually "safer" victims than men. Many women are left vulnerable when their husbands are away on business trips or working late. (It is not uncommon for an intruder to watch a house for days, learning the male's habits, "casing" when a female or a child is alone.) If a burglar gets into your house, he may be deterred from getting into your bedroom if the type of lock used on the bedroom door is the same quality used on exterior doors. If the resident hears an intruder coming through a hallway, the bedroom lock can add precious time to a potential victim's defense. It allows time to call for help.

Don't worry about police officers or firefighters not being able to get through your bedroom door in the event of an emergency . . . they get through tougher doors and locks every day *by force*. Fire companies carry axes and other devices for defeating home barriers when they are fighting fires. Police and fire personnel are not worried about making noise, awakening the resident, or causing an alarm. (If they do *not* try to get past a barrier to take care of an emergency, they most certainly haven't been keeping up with news about litigations.)

"KICK-IN" HOME ASSAULTS

When a door or its frame is not sturdy, a burglar or determined assailant can come through the door by sheer force. This is called a "kick-in" crime. Police kick in doors all the time, and criminals do so, as well. Incidents of reported kick-in entries are increasing. If your home is not built like a fortress and you feel threatened, get certain doors reinforced. A bolt for a good lock should be, at a minimum, one inch long and made of tempered steel. A crook can get through a pin tumbler lock by kicking the door, *if* the metal in the lock is not strong enough. *They will break.* Strength, as well as design, is why some locks are more expensive than others.

It is also possible to force an entire lock out of its housing. Criminals have been known, on many occasions, to simply place the teeth of a large wrench around the lock and pry it out of the housing. A deterrent is made by placing a strong metal plate around the lock, with no screws or bolts visible to the outside. If your lock has a circular design that molds toward the surface of the door, you can install a metal collar, called a "slip ring," that makes it near-impossible for a criminal to get a wrench around the lock. The slip ring was designed to rotate under the wrench's force, while protecting the lock.

Kick-in attacks are not restricted to exterior or entry doors. They can be directed toward an interior door in a home, specifically the bedroom door. Precautions against kick-in attacks also should be taken with interior doors.

To guard against "kick-in" burglaries, there are items on the market that "harden the target" against such incidents. The MAG company of Gardena, California, advertises that several of their products strengthen the part of the door that takes the attackers force—the striker plate on the door jamb and the door area directly around the deadbolt lock. The Uni-Force is a heavy-duty metal sleeve that surrounds the door where the deadbolt projects, while the Strike-3 Deadbolt and Frame Reinforcer is advertised to more than double the strength of the strike. The company's Install-A-Lock is supposed to prevent kick-in attacks, but it can decrease damage and save costly door replacement. Everyone has seen movies where New York flats, have five big locks on one door. It looks silly, but Vessels says this practice is a sound idea. A number of good locks on a solid core door, with an equally strong frame and plate, spreads the stress on the door. Sturdy and strong, the door has less chance of giving way to force.

HOW MUCH SHOULD YOU PAY FOR LOCKS?

There is a correlation between security provided and the cost of locks. A good lock will be manufactured of the strongest materials. It will be finely made with close tolerances and will be resistent to tampering, manipulation, or picking. A good lock will be fairly sophisticated inside, compared to a cheaper lock. Most important, with today's soaring crime rates, violent family breakups, and a large drug culture seeking more money than most people earn, locks alone are not enough to ensure personal security.

It can be argued that if you are installing locks that will protect you from physical attack, no cost is too much to bear. If you are putting on locks to protect inexpensive property stored inside a near-empty shed, then heavy-duty, expensive locks would not be the answer. The cost of locks must generally equate to the threat-level against which you seek protection.

Getting What You Pay For

According to Tom Vessels, a person in the market for a good locksmith should shop around, compare reputations, and talk to satisfied customers. Some of the more credible locksmiths are members of ALOA, the Association of Locksmiths Of

America. Headquartered in Texas, Vessels says it is one of the most advanced associations for locksmiths. They have PRP tests—Proficiency Registration Program. "I think some of the questions on the tests are silly," Vessels says, "such as 'Which color line do you attach first?' But, it's good because it stops some of the people who don't know the business.

"In locks, you get what you pay for," Vessels says. "We put a KWIKSET 660 model, which is a light-duty model, on a two-by-two board. We put the 880 model on a two-by-two board. The second lock you can't find at a discount store. It's a heavy-duty lock, not in their market. We took a crowbar and a twenty-ounce framing hammer to them. One lick with the framing hammer and the light model was torn off the door, and we were able to reach in with only a fingernail and pull the bolt back. The heavy-duty model stayed on that door. We had a guy pound on it for fifteen minutes, until he was exhausted. I had a trainee in here who said he could get it off. He went out and pounded on it for ten more minutes. The wood was destroyed, but the lock was still intact."

The price for this Superman lock? "KWIKSET 880 lock. About thirty-five dollars for a single cylinder. That's a good lock. As far as picking this lock, they are easy to pick, but professionalism is dying. Nobody is picking locks anymore. They're breaking windows."

Are there any other locks that Vessels would recommend? Yes, but with reservations. He likes some models by SCHLAGE but cautions that many locks that used to be of high quality are no longer. They are being foreign made with cheaper, weaker metal and the insides of the locks are less skillfully made.

"They are using a lower grade of pot metal," he said. "I know, because I've beaten them up to test them. And when we go to replace locks, such as a deadbolt in a storage room, and my guys go in and have to drill it . . . the better quality SCHLAGE locks, we *have* to drill. The lower quality, the burglars get through."

BURGLARS, LOCKS, TIN-SNIPS, AND WINDOWS

What do burglars look for and how do you foil locks? "It depends on whom you are defending against. If you have a five-hundred pound guy smacking into the door, either YALE 'finger' locks or deadbolts will give way because the door itself will give way. The locks are usually much stronger than the door frames.

"Another thing," Vessels explains. "You know on your garage doors? The regular sliding bolt? The mentality of a burglar is why waste time going for this big lock with this half-inch hardened shackle through it. The piece you are locking it through is less than 1/8 inch of mild, zinc-coated tin. His answer is to take a tin-snip and cut through that simple little piece. Also, some of the smartest burglars won't even mess with doors. They go through walls. A smart burglar is going to be smart enough to get in. Some of them simply remove the glass in a window; they don't break it. They take out the lining and use suction cups to lift out the glass pane. You never hear it."

Vessels advises putting longer screws into the stud next to the striker plate, making a deadbolt stronger into the wood. First, find the stud next to the door. It's usually not more than an inch back. "But, I've seen some Harvey Homeowner construction where I can't even find a stud back there," Vessels says. "You feel kinda' sad when you are putting a lock on a door and you can't find a stud back there. Then, all the guy has locking his door is a 3/4 inch by 1/2 inch piece of pine.

"There are some simple precautions you can take against burglars who make keys for your locks." Vessels recommends filing numbers off locks. Keep a record somewhere. "They are now putting the numbers on with ink, so you need a pencil eraser. I'm now seeing MASTER padlocks with the numbers only on the keys, not on the locks."

Another way to prevent theft is to require that people desiring duplicate keys complete a form, just in case a burglary or theft follows. "People will come in and say, 'Can you cut me a key to this master?' I say, 'Sure, fill out this form.' You don't have liability as a locksmith. I've had people turn around and walk out. It makes me feel good. The local police department had their garage ripped off and went to another locksmith for assistance. The other guy chased the detective out of his shop, yelling, 'I don't have to take that information down, it's not the law.' So, I've been doing business with that police department for a long time, now." Vessels says that about 95 percent of his business is after the fact, *after* people have been burglarized . . . or worse. "People aren't prepared."

How much does it cost to re-do all the locks in a house these days? When Vessels was eighteen, the deadbolt craze was on. "Everybody was getting deadbolts," he says. "We'd do all the doors and windows in a house for one-hundred-fifty dollars. Now, you're looking at four- to five-hundred dollars to do the same job. Like locks, times have sure changed."

· **11** ·

Dennis

If you are a woman, or you have sisters, a mother, a female companion or a wife living in your home, it is important that you meet Dennis. Dennis is a "smarter than your average bear" rapist and kidnapper. He is in maximum security prison in a northern state. Prior to that incarceration, he was imprisoned in the South where he escaped twice, leading state police on dramatic chases through forests, along rivers and, in one instance, where he reputedly flew to safety in a stolen airplane. Dennis has raped a lot of women, and he claims to be repentent. He has agreed to bare his lifestyle, prior to incarceration, to help women who read this book be safe.

1. How did you choose the victims?

"I would drive around and watch for women who would be driving alone or walking alone. If I saw them go to what appeared to be their residence, I would wait and watch. In the event that the residence was an apartment complex, I would observe the apartment the potential victim would enter. Then I would look at mailboxes and note whether this individual was listed as a first and last name (being a woman's name), or whether there was just a first initial and a last name. The latter would pose more of a risk, as I would not know whether the initial stood for a male. Therefore, if I was determined to capitalize on the woman, I would observe her for a few days, in between other victims. The woman would generally be attractive to me, although out of desperation, I have settled for less attrac-

tive women, to satisfy my need for sex. It is the consensus
that most rapists commit their crimes as acts of violence
against women. That was not the case with me. I needed
sex. My wife could not satisfy me due to her working and
sleeping. As hard as that may seem, it is the truth. I was shy
around women, and was unable to set up dates simply for
sex. You should also know, that I was continually using
drugs."

2. How did you get into homes and cars?

"Homes seemed to be the safer place, as they posed less risk
of my being seen by someone I would be unaware of at the
time. However, I have taken advantage of a situation
where the vehicle became the place of my crime. In that
case, I would drive or have the victim drive to a secluded
area, take care of my business, and drive the victim back to
where I picked her up, or in the case of a hitch-hiker, I
would drop her off where she wanted. Risky, on my part, as
I made the mistake of my car being identified.

"As for the residence of a victim, night hours were the best
opportunity to seize control. With the lights on in the residence, I could take advantage of seeing inside, with mini-
mal chance of being seen by anyone in the dwelling. I
would first note whether I could be seen by someone who
may be looking out a window of a next door residence, or
who would happen to walk or drive by the area. The darker
the outside of the dwelling, the better. These would be
houses that could be cased with less chance of being seen.
As for apartments, I used a different approach, such as
going to the door, knocking, and hoping a woman opened
the door. Once she did, then I could push myself inside
under threat of injury. I would use a knife, as they (knives)
are perceived as being quiet, and the victim could not use
the noise that a gun would make as an advantage. The
threat of injury, in my case, was a bluff. If it looked like it
may come to injuring someone, I would leave and find
another victim. This, however, should not set the
precedence for all rapists. The idea of gaining access to the
dwelling was to lead a woman to believe that I was in need
of assistance, such as looking for someone, saying that I
damaged a car, or something of that nature. Making it look
like an innocent matter. Someone in need of help.

3. What would you advise women to do, to protect themselves from rapists?

"First, women should become more cognizant of their situation when alone. It doesn't matter if they are married or not. She can still become a victim to a very terrible crime. For instance, let's say a woman is at home, and her husband is at work. I come to the door seeking help for what I make out to be an emergency situation. I would inquire as to whether her husband could offer me assistance. A woman should never say that her husband is not home at the time. I inquire further, as to whether someone else could offer assistance. In the case her answer is "no," as to her husband being home, then I inquire if anyone else is in the building? Once I am satisfied that she is alone, I make my move by getting her to invite me in to use the telephone, etc., or I force my way in under threat of harm. I may not even make my move at that time. I simply case the place for a few days.

"Second, women should always drive with the car doors locked. It is nothing, for someone to simply walk up, open the door and enter the car. Once inside, they can pull a knife and have her drive to a designated spot.

"Third, women who live alone should never put their full names on a mailbox. That is an indication they live alone. This is generally in apartments, although houses are targets too. This is one of the major mistakes women make. Why give someone information that can be used against you?

"Fourth, in the case that a woman is being raped and it looks like she has no way out of it, her best option would be not to anger the offender, as he may do whatever is necessary to make her submissive to his advances. In some cases, she may be successful in fighting off her offender. That is risky and could be life-threatening, depending on the profile of the individual committing the crime. Some people are more violent than others. That's why rape from a stranger is so unpredictable as to the amount of injury that may be inflicted. There could be a difference with date rape, where the victim knows her attacker.

The attacker would not want to risk being identified to the police and there would be generally less violence involved. Her coming out alive with as little injury as possible should be the primary concern, even if it means being passive and submissive. Depending on the situation, taking mental notes of her attacker for follow-up is very important. The bottom line is that a rape victim should bring her attacker to justice, as he may case her for another attack. In the event that he is watching her for such an attack and he sees the police at the scene, then chances are he is going to give up on her and leave the area.

"I am not advocating lying, but under these circumstances a woman could prevent herself from being raped by saying that she was diagnosed as having a contagious disease. It does work as a defense in some cases.

"These are merely a few examples for women to take preventative measures. I do want to help. This is the first real chance I have had to help women who might be victims, and I really feel good about it."

Respectfully,

Dennis

According to the April 23, 1992 report, "Rape in America," compiled by the National Victim Center and the Crime Victims Research and Treatment Center of the Department of Psychiatry and Behavioral Sciences at Medical University, in Charleston, South Carolina, there are 683,00 rapes per year; 1.3 per minute; 78 an hour; 56,916 per month; 1,871 per day. The study's definition of rape? "An event that occurs without the woman's consent, involving the use of force or threat of force, and involving sexual penetration of the victim's vagina, mouth or rectum." Women were asked whether such experiences had occurred anytime during their lifetimes, whether or not they reported it to police, and whether the attacker was a stranger, family member, boyfriend, or friend. The study focused *only* on forcible rape of women. Clearly all types of sexual assault do not involve force, so the numbers in the study, however frightening, may be very conservative.

According to the study, one out of every eight adult women, or at least 12.1 million American women has been a victim of forcible rape sometime in her lifetime. Over 29 percent were raped before the age of 11 years old. Thirty-two percent were raped between the ages of 11 and 17 years old. Twenty-two percent of the forcible rapes occurred between the ages of 18 and 24. The rest of the percentages were spread rather evenly throughout the women's age groups. Nearly 40 percent of the women studied had been victims of more than one sexual assault. It's a fact that women simply are not safe in this country.

(Results are from *The National Women's Study,* funded by the National Institute of Drug Abuse, a three-year longitudinal study of a national probability sample of 4,008 adult women. In *The State of Services for Victims of Rape,* a study sponsored by the National Victim Center, 370 agencies that provide crisis assistance to rape victims were survey respondents. In the second study, not all victims who responded had reported the rapes to police.)

All the Security
Money Can Buy

In the late Eighties, an experienced, street-savvy police officer lamented that *both* the extremely rich and the extremely poor are now prisoners. "In the inner-city," he said, "residents live in the backs of their houses to avoid the 'drive-by' shootings. They're afraid to go out at night. The rich live in barricaded fortresses. They spend a fortune protecting all they have." Indeed, the wealthy are seeking better hardware and keener expertise to be, or at least *feel*, safe. Come with us, as we study the secrets behind protecting those "champagne and caviar dreams."

In our search for the finest "high-end" security-design architects, we found that most architects depend upon the advice of security experts to design a safe home. The problem we found is that an "expert" is in the eye of the beholder. In an analysis of homes in over thirty cities, we repeatedly found homes where tremendous amounts of money had been spent on gates that wouldn't keep people out, fences teenagers could climb over, and seeming "fortresses" that would bring an instant smile to a burglar's face. In our search for the right architects, we discovered a unique, and possibly a "one-of-a-kind" custom security designer. His name was Jeff Sulkin. And Jeff Sulkin designs "high-end" homes for the famous and very, *very* rich.

What makes Sulkin unique? His upbringing and his number one consultant, a father who for 30 years designed "top secret" government projects. "In my childhood," Sulkin said, "I was never once allowed in my father's office." Now semi-retired, Sulkin's father has a room in the rear portion of his son's array of open-air, design work-spaces in Santa Monica, California. Do you want to survive a riot or the worst of enemies who is out to get you? Or do you simply want to protect your multi-million-dollar art collection from thieves? Sulkin and Associates has an edge when it comes to security design. They are the best we've seen. Glean what you can from someone who solves security problems with architectural design.

THE PRODUCER

"The Producer" works in the film industry. What he buys and where he lives is all a part of his standing in his profession. He is a very prominent art collector, and he now had too much art for the wall space he had available. He didn't want to move. He wanted to continue buying art while keeping all he owns.

"No matter what we built," Sulkin said, "we could *never* have built a big enough building on his narrow sloping site. If we could have, it would have been a gigantic structure that no one would have wanted to live in. It would have been like living in a commercial building."

Sulkin devised a plan to put the producer's art collection on the third story of the house. The problem was how to get new art up there without a stranger coming into the house. "Contemporary artists use very, *very* big canvases," Sulkin said. "Nine-by-nine, ten-by-fourteen. It's always a big headache. Some are very heavy, some are even made of cement."

Sulkin devised "flexible, modular, moving, swinging, sliding wall panels." The panel moves, rather than the object attached to it. "There is nothing to screw, nothing to lock, no levers." Sulkin said. "Six-hundred pounds of weight is supported on a one-inch ball bearing on one end." Sulkin calls it his "Arcsystem." And what does this have to do with security?

The producer wants to be able to call and say, "I'm coming back Wednesday and I'm bringing a new painting. Move that painting off the wall and take it to storage. Put the new one in its place." If something is shipped, he may not know the day it will come. Will it sit in a warehouse? Will it be wrapped properly? What if he is on a business trip when it arrives? Under no circumstances, does he want strangers in his house.

How does the new painting enter the house? The delivery van comes to the bottom floor driveway and the driver pushes a combination onto a keypad. A door automatically slides open, high above on the third floor. A harness beam moves out, and a cable drops. The truckdriver hooks the painting crate onto the cable and presses the keypad again. The crate goes up, goes in, and the door closes. It's all automatic. The van driver leaves.

"Now the painting is in the storage room, three stories up," Sulkin said. And what if the truckdriver decides he can hook himself up and hoist *himself* into the producer's house? The delivery room is sealed off. No one can get into the house from the delivery room without an insider allowing entry.

MR X

"Mr. X" has a house below grade, at the end of a long, sloping driveway. He wants to block the view of his house from the street. He also wants to be able to see who is at his gate. He doesn't want to depend on security cameras alone, which can malfunction.

Sulkin designed a small but beautiful tower that has a glass dome of intricate European design. It fulfills both aesthetic and security purposes: a tall entrance to the house, and an inside mirror that works like a periscope. At all times, the homeowner can see his gate a few hundred feet away. What if an intruder tries to break through the glass dome? He would exhaust himself for nothing. The dome has steel-frame ribs with small openings, none large enough for even a small burglar to get through. Instead of typical leaded glass windows, this dome has ribs that are 1/16 of an inch thick, very tiny, but they are two-inches deep. From below, the dome has a delicate pattern, from above it is remarkably strong. It is a grill. "There is a second dome over that one," Sulkin says, "And that one is acrylic." In addition, if anyone walks across the floor of the entry hall, an electric eye lights the dome. "Most people hate bars on the windows," Sulkin says. "It is my job to find another way to give them security. You don't always have to solve security problems mechanically, with hardware. You can solve them architecturally."

THE FOUR-RATED ROOM

"Mrs. Ritz" was a very prominent businesswoman who owned a big chunk of a major corporation. She willed her priceless porcelain collection to one of the most prestigeous museums in the world. For this grand deed, she was given a sizable tax break. A requirement of the agreement was that the porcelain collection had to be protected in a vault with a fire and security rating of 4, the highest available. The museum was making a space for the famed collection, and they wanted no thefts, no accidents.

Jeff Sulkin outfitted a projection room in Mrs. Ritz's home with four walls and a ceiling of steel. "If you've been in the Los Angeles riot zone," Sulkin pointed out, "you noticed the steel beams bent over. When steel is on fire in a contained area, it will melt, no matter how strong it is. The space for the porcelain had to provide enough air space around the room, to dispense heat, drain heat. There was also a vent in the floor. We put wooden panels over everything, and finally, we added the bank vault door which cost five thousand dollars."

Beautiful wood also was placed over the bank vault door to make it more genteel. The walls that adjoined the door had to be structured wide enough to fit. Mrs. Ritz's entire projection room became an elegant vault.

MR. PROPRIETY'S BATHROOM

"Mr. Propriety" wanted a safe place to escape if he were away from his bedroom area and his safe room. He didn't want his safe in the master bedroom because that location was too obvious to intruders. In addition, he requested design modifications to the bathroom off his dining room area. He didn't want someone to leave the table to go to the bathroom and have everyone at his party hear the conversation between the person *in* the bathroom and the person *wanting* to get into the bathroom. It isn't refined.

How do the two needs work together, security and privacy? Quite nicely. Sulkin designed a doorknob with a slide bolt. When a person enters and turns the latch, the entire bolt disappears into the wall. Nothing is visible. It no longer looks like a door; it looks like a wall, and there is no way to get in. "You don't have a whole conversation within earshot of everyone eating dinner. And as a safe room, you can escape in there and no one will even realize there is a room there. When there is no handle, an intruder passes by." The door and the room seem to disappear. Now, that's security.

13

The Psychology of
Security Design

JEFF SULKIN, ARCHITECT

"There is a psychology to the way anyone looks at a structure. Is it heavy, light, impenetrable? An example is
Stonehenge. Stonehenge is an astronomical observatory,
but the geometry of that building and, the sighting devices
it incorporates, could have been done with popsicle sticks.
The reason it is that big is not because it was meant to last a
long time. There is imagery at work that goes beyond the
function it was to accomplish. The priests wanted an impregnability. *That* is a principle used in security design.

"You can make a wall angled and sloped; make it look
heavy like an old embattlement. You can make slit windows. Give a sense of depth to the structure. If you have
gates, you paint them black instead of white. There is a
psychology to all of that. In dealing with the initial impression you get when you look at a home . . . whether it's a
criminal or *you* getting that impression . . . there is a
whole series of visual cues. For a look of heaviness, you use
textures, stone materials or stone veneers.

"You control the view line. You can't really see into a wall,
you can only see a 'peek'. How many openings are there?
Are the windows recessed making the walls look thick? Can
you see through the front gate? All of these elements helps a

criminal get a sudden impression, and most crime is for-mulated on a snap decision. Criminals know how long they want to spend inside a building. They want to get in and get out. If I were a criminal trying to select a house to burgle, and I saw thick walls and heavy-set windows, all those cues, and I also saw a house with little Colonial-paned windows and thin doors, wood siding, I would prob-ably choose the second one. If I saw locks that are enlarged with big safe plates on the doors, that wouldn't be the one I'd pick. I'd go to the next facade.

"Consider the bag of tricks architects can use in security design: Elements that make you think of impregnability, also make you think of *weight*. If those elements are used on the front facade or visible areas of a corner building, they will give pause to someone who might want to get in. For instance, if you use stone trim around windows, it makes it harder to chip out a window. Whether it is practical is not even the point. How does it make a potential intruder initially feel?

"Also of issue is the massing of the building, whether there are a lot of nooks and crannies, recessed entrance-ways, places to hide. If you want to eliminate that issue, don't use those elements at the front of the house. You don't want any place for a person to hide. There are enough traditional elements that have a sense of weight so you can work with traditional style and still have security.

"Certain styles of houses are more delicate looking and are harder to work with, but even a Victorian home with wood trim can look stronger by accentuating the wood trim. That's a proportion game. A large house with French coun-try trim can still give the impression of weight.

"It is easier to design modern homes for security. Large, plate glass windows are now very thick. Most criminals don't want to break them. They can even be dangerous. Instead, criminals will go for small panes, access panels and doors. French doors are not great. The weakest part of the door is the wood, not the glass. You can break the wood. When I design them, I make the moldings thicker and use steel frames. You also use heavier grade silicons, making it harder to cut through the joints. If you use enough silicon in the glass door, the glass won't come apart. You can rip parts of the woodwork, but the glass stays in place. That means extra care in design, extra cost.

"In most university courses, they hit security design very little. I've had to learn a lot from my clients. Someone will come in and say, 'We've been burglarized three times, and each time they came through the French doors.' The practical, life-solving problems of a house are not being addressed in school. Security design is neglected. Will you be imprisoned by your security system, for instance? What if you have a dog or cat and you can't use laser alarms? How do you make someone *feel* protected?

"You don't have to be rich to have a secure home. Security can be affordable by simply dealing with the classic elements of architecture. Vision through the space, or how landscaping is handled, is very important. Whether you can see around your home depends upon how the walls are laid out. There are hundreds of years of philosophy about how to do that. The Roman courtyards are wonderful. The original Ghetty Museum in Malibu, California was designed as a courtyard. You can look into any door. Obviously, because of climate, you might not be able to have that design in Buffalo, New York, but the principal applies that you can have any part of the house visually accessible from one point."

14

Three Urban Fortresses

WHAT CAN BE LEARNED

Too often, security is a consideration *after* a crime has occurred or *after* a house is built. That is the most expensive and troublesome route to making your home safe. In this chapter, we spotlight three homes where security was a major design priority, *before* a foundation ever was poured. Each home was designed by a different architect, each having a different approach to making a house secure.

The first, by Randy Morris, is an impenetrable fortress on an inland waterway. Wide beachfront sidewalks invite "inlanders" from volatile neighborhoods in less affluent areas, to spend evenings sightseeing in this wealthy area. The police department in this city is severely under-resourced and the crime rate is very high, though the neighborhoods are charming. The family that lives in the Morris house claims not to be afraid; they shouldn't be. Their home is built like a veritable "rock house," though its expanses of glass make it seem open and airy.

The second, designed by American architect Jeff Sulkin and built for an American businessman, blends into the ancient architecture of Israel, a country with a history of terrorism and political upheaval. The need for security design in this home is neither folly nor needless expense. It is serious business, and in some instances, living defensively through security design is reflected in Israel's building codes themselves.

The third is the suburban home of an inventer and engineer, and his well-known socialite wife, who for her bounty of charity work boasts her own Oscar. The house overlooks a deep canyon in a gated community that has virtually no crime, although it is few miles from the crime-ridden areas of a major American city. Designed by Edward Carson Beall, security in this home is unobtrusive, though dependant on sophisticated gadgetry that is quite expensive. Although the average homeowner may not be able to afford the security systems on the Beall home, the house offers an opportunity to show state-of-the-art security features currently available.

Randy Morris—European Shutters

It is relatively easy to spot a Randy Morris house. His elegant and very expensive homes have huge, towering sheets of glass. Although they appear open and unforbidding, a second study reveals Morris houses are cleverly "closed down" to intruders or even unwelcome visitors. They are the homes on the block with lots of sheen, light and high-tech surfaces, but to an intruder, they scream, "Go away. *No one* can get in here."

Although Morris usually designs contemporary houses, he claims most of his clients think traditionally designed homes afford less security design opportunity. "That isn't true," Morris says. "Actually, you can include *more* security elements with traditional design than with contemporary design. In Spanish style you can use grills. They don't have to look like barred windows. They can have flavor and style. And you can do a lot with shutters."

Morris points out that many clients no longer want French doors, which are easy to penetrate, although any choice of window is possible, *if* you can afford it. He recalls designing one house where the windows had steel "break-ups." If someone wanted to break in, he would have had to use a blowtorch." Wooden windows, which are relatively inexpensive, will not deter a burglar. Steel windows add about 20 percent to the cost, according to Morris. On his "Urban Fortress," spotlighted in this chapter, he incorporated huge security shutters over security windows.

"You close the European shutters on this home and go away," he explains. "European shutters are also good for sun and breeze control. It's a great way to shut your house down. They are hand-cranked with a pulley system, and they are usually an 'add-on.' In other countries they are built right in, and they are attractive. You see them all over South America. I am amazed we don't see more of them here."

Morris thought of using the shutters while on a walk during a raging sea storm. He stood on the public sidewalk near the building site and braved a 100 MPH wind. "And I'll tell you, during that storm, *everything* leaked. The shutters protect against that kind of threat, as well. They are steel framed with steel panels. Because the home faces the sea, the shutters had to be protected from salt spray. They were stripped and painted at an area boatyard with special undercoating of epoxy and a coat of polyurathene. The paint job cost four-thousand dollars, and five pairs of two-story-high shutters cost seventeen-thousand dollars. The large windows they protect are twin-pane, for both security and environmental control.

To further "harden the target," Morris added a Rixon lock, installed on the one magnificent door on the ground floor. A Rixon lock is a deadbolt lock with a hook. As it comes into the slot, it hooks into the steel frame. The Rixon lock doesn't cost any more than any other high-quality deadbolt lock.

Why twin-pane glass? Tempered glass is too easily broken with a pointed object. "A pointed object releases the pressure and the window shatters and falls away in granules," Morris says. Unfortunately, the boldness of crooks is changing. Noise no longer drives a burglar away."

A hint for homeowners who live close to curbside, Morris suggests a number of barriers in the security design, one element hidden by another. "And it doesn't aesthetically have to look like a fortress," he claims. His barrier design idea came from a commercial client who wanted a building "where no one could back through a plate-glass window and drive away with the store." (This request was made long before the 1992 Los Angeles riots.) Such barriers can be incorporated easily into existing homes. Architects wanting to gain ideas for such designs need only study plans for newer police stations in urban areas. Most have attractive barriers to prevent an irate citizen from driving through the front doors and right into the lobby.

Jeff Sulkin—Bluff-Top Haven

Jeff Sulkin's house on the bluff overlooks a 2,000-year-old Roman aqueduct in Israel. While its design respects the history of the area, it also looks impregnable. In the house on the bluff, little is mere image. The house is made of concrete. It is, as the client demanded, "one-thousand percent fireproof." Along with blending in with the ancient history of the aqueduct, the client wanted a playhouse. He has four children. Children don't run in straight lines. He wanted large open areas where the children could run around and through.

"The entire inside of the house is Ceasar stone," Sulkin says. "He wanted stonework on the floor, a softness of white. The building itself follows the shape of the hill. The openings of the breezeways are large, allowing the clients to see the whole yard and the entire terrace. That was a security consideration."

From the terrace, the client wanted to view the beauty of the ancient aqueduct, though there was need for a solid parapet. Either Sulkin had to give up the terrace or have an unsafe terrace where someone could shoot at his client. What he did was cast the concrete ceiling in circular steps. On the terrace above, if the client sits on the top level, he can see the aqueduct. If someone comes, or danger approaches, he can move to a lower level for safety. It is a simple, common sense design.

Another problem with desert homes is that they tend to be very dark as a protection against scorching sun. Skylights are popular, but with skylights there are waterproofing problems, as well as security concerns. Sulkin opted for round glass blocks cast directly into the ceiling. They are impregnable and fireproof, since they are constructed of multiple layers of glass. There are light bulbs in the ceiling near the glass blocks. In the evening, the client can flick a switch, and the beautiful sunlight pattern of the day lights up the room at night.

The building is set back on the bluff, and the feeling is solid. There is nowhere to hide. Anyone who wanders close can be seen by the clients before that person sees them. An interesting element is the design of the safe room in the house on the bluff. The client is an Orthodox Jew. He requires a Mikvah, the ritual bath, if it became necessary that he sequester himself from danger. Sulkin designed a spa/bath/gymnasium/safe room where the client can take his ritual bath, regardless of the danger surrounding him and his family.

Ed Beall—The House with Eyes and Ears

Ed Beall designed a house with eyes and ears for Chuck and Carol Drexel. Drexel, an inventor and engineer, wanted a home that would be both beautiful and enduring, "that would last into the next century." Security was simply one more element of quality; yet it was not at the top of the list of the Drexel's priorities. They dislike security that intrudes, either on their lives or upon the comfort of guests.

Beall's design incorporated an indoor shooting range, a spacious gym, large rooms with city lights views and no electrical outlets in sight. Chuck Drexel, a handsome grey-haired intellectual, insisted his home have only unevenly molded walls. Not one wall is boring and flat. Outside, as the sun moves across the sky, silver minnows appear to swim through the pool, an optical illusion designed by architect Beall, who also painted the large mural in the master bedroom. This is a dream home hard-won by a dream couple, and the house is a symbol of their maturity, success and refinement. Unfortunately, the Drexels quality of life needs protection in today's America. To do the job, Beall incorporated "top of the line" electronic gadgetry into the home's security design.

The house and grounds are monitored by seven television cameras. You cannot see them. The lenses look like tiny black flies on the walls. All peek out unobtrusively and all are linked to indoor monitors that can be watched from every room. Inside, guests would have to search for the monitors. The monitors, too, are unobtrusive. A small microphone monitors all sounds outside in the pool area. "We had that put in to hear the children," Carol Drexel said, "in case of emergency." An added benefit: while Mrs. Drexel is in the kitchen, the detection system also pulls in the charm of birdcalls in the canyon and the peaceful gurgling of a nearby stream.

The guestrooms have electronic security systems inside the headboards of the beds. One bedroom was designed for an invalid. Security features, lights, drapes, stereo and television can be controlled from that single station. The buttons are very large. A frail person can't miss them.

In the master bedroom, a television screen monitors all doors and windows in the house. Downstairs, a second larger screen scans the entire house for fires. Lights on a sophisticated annunciator board notify if and where a fire starts. An added feature: it is possible to call the house from thousands of miles away to direct computer generated activity, making the home look inhabited at any time of the day. Bright lighting is integral to the security design. "Electricians joked that if all the lights went on in this house at once, the lights of nearby cities would dim," Mrs. Drexel said. There are 250 lights in the ceiling, for security. The Drexels are environmentally conservative. They do not use them unless there is an emergency.

The Drexel home is located in a gated community, well-posted with an especially large, parking lot sign that reads "Sheriff." There are twenty-four hour staffings of guard posts. In our security test to reach the Drexels either by phone or simply to gain their address, we had not a shred of success. Under *no* circumstances did the security force reveal anything about the Drexels, even when pressed with official sounding requests, and later, pleading.

SECURITY SHUTTERS

The average homeowner may not be able to afford two-story-high shutters over specialty glass, although shutters are becoming a common security up-grade, even for condominiums. Security shutters are currently the major security "add-ons" after installation of burglar alarms. If there are home association rules forbidding attaching them to the outside of units, rolling shutters can be easily affixed to the inside. They are hidden beneath padded valences that blend into the overall decorating scheme.

Consumers should get several bids before contracting for shutter up-grades. An ethical salesperson will use discretion, making recommendations when family members have disabilities. A warning: as paranoia about crime has grown, security features have become a hot product in the housing market. A number of vendors have entered the security business with little more than venture capital.

There have been consumer complaints about vendors not being able to provide warranty services. Others have quickly gone out of business. Check on the record of a shutter business. Can they provide warranty service? Will they refer you to customers? How many years have they been in business?

Shutters are excellent security features that also provide temperature and breeze control. They enable a house to be shut down and present the ultimate psychological effect of a hardened target.

If you are disabled or in frail health, before buying shutters, make sure you have the physical strength to hand-crank them down if electrical power fails.

· 15 ·

Victimization at the Hands of Hired Help

Police logs list numerous crimes committed by employees in the home or temporary employees who make calls to homes. These crimes include everything from kidnapping a baby and stealing outdoor vegetation for sale at swap meets to setting the family up for relatives to burgle. Don't be paranoid about such incidents happening to you. There are many decent, hard-working maids, rug cleaners and wallpaper hangers who are respectable and honest. However, there are ways to reduce your chances of being victimized by the home employees who seek you out as prey.

The private non-profit, National Crime Prevention Council in Washington, DC, aided in the writing of this chapter. The National Crime Prevention Council acts as a national clearing house for crime prevention, and they own the registration to McGruff, the anti-crime dog ("Take a bite out of crime.") used in Neighborhood Watch literature. Jean F. O'Neil was the spokesperson. She has some excellent information to share.

HONESTY TESTS

Honesty tests are becoming popular in business since the polygraph test is so controversial—often considered an invasion of a person's rights and documented as not being reliable. Regardless of how much money a homeowner has to spend, private persons usually can't acquire honesty tests, which many corporations are using to replace the polygraph for employee screening.

"Most honesty tests are propriety instruments or are licensed instruments," O'Neil says. "There are some great honesty tests, but in order to get copies, the licensee may want thousands of dollars. Also, honesty tests are not normally purchased." Honesty tests also require expert interpretation, for which the average homeowner is not trained. It is possible, however, for a homeowner to contract for drug testing of potential employees, or during periods of employment, just as businesses do.

Bringing Service Employees into Your Home

If you need a cleaning service or home repairs, check out companies with the Better Business Bureau and your Chamber of Commerce. Ask if there have been complaints, not so much concerning the quality of work but about other problems. You also may check with the local police department. Make sure the companies you want to hire are licensed. Many people set themselves up in business and never get a license. "You would want someone who is stable enough to be properly licensed," O'Neil said, "*and* bonded."

Bonding is a form of insurance. The owner of a maid service or home repair company will go to an agent to have employees cleared, or bonded. Then, if those employees steal, or if they are the cause of a loss of valuables, the company is covered for those losses, *up to a certain ceiling amount*. It is important to know that ceiling amount. How do you know if a company is bonded? According to our inquiries, most homeowner hiring and employee screening is handled over the telephone, where potential clients have no proof of bonding. Surprisingly, most clients never ask for that proof. It is within your rights as a customer to ask for written proof of bonding.

An inherent problem with bonding is that no amount of money can replace certain items. The loss of heirlooms or "sentimental value" items, such as grandmother's engagement ring, is an emotional loss. Decide, *before* you have hired help come into your home, what you can't bear to lose. Many clients allow cleaning personnel to clean a home while they are not there. If that is how your cleaning hours must be scheduled, secure family heirlooms, small "pocketable" items, and easily-fenced articles. Or, have a trusted friend or relative supervise the cleaning in your absence.

Be aware; there are other limits to bonding. Bonding, in most cases, means the criminal history of an employee has been checked, *but* a company only may be concerned if a potential employee has committed theft or has been fired for stealing, not whether he or she has been accused of child molesting or a violent crime during a drunken spree. KNOW WHAT THE BOND COVERS. Does it cover only quality of work? Does it cover the employee causing injury to someone else while working on your property? Does it cover theft, damage? Ask. If you are not happy with the answers, find another company.

A company should be willing to show you a written bonding policy or a copy of the bond itself. The policy probably will be written in "legal-ese," and the bond itself most certainly will. But, make sure you read it. A state agency for consumer affairs or your state attorney general's office may be able to give you information about the state requirements for bonding. In some states, certain professions require bonding.

Ask the company representative how long the company has been in business. Ask for written references. May you contact these people or businesses? If a reference says something such as, "Mr. Smith is a nice person and I liked him very much," realize those words say nothing about the work habits or product of Mr. Smith *or* the standard of his character.

During stressed economic times, many people "moonlight" doing home service work, such as cleaning windows, home-fixit chores, and low-grade landscaping. Many of those ads are carried in "throw-away" newspapers. When you are trying to save yourself money, remember one thing—you get what you pay for. When it comes to security issues, it's usually true. According to spokespersons at the National Crime Prevention Council, more cities should offer a service such as "The Checkbook," which is available in the Metro area of Washington, DC. It lists information about home service companies— the approval ratings, reliability and quality of work. It is a non-profit organization, consumer-driven, and apparently very effective and much appreciated.

Jean O'Neil cautions on those services, although she considers "The Checkbook" quite good. "You can have a client who may find a worker was very charming and reminded her of her grandson," O'Neil said. "The fact that he was there two hours longer than necessary escaped notice. I may have a meeting to attend, and the same adorable young man who comes to repair my sink will make me late. There is an issue of quality in these surveys, sometimes. . . . but not honesty of workers. Most people who take part in ratings services are knowledgable people."

O'Neil advises that homeowners go to the reference librarian of their local library, a "low-cost source of information about home repair, maid services and workers' compensation."

When working with a contractor who sends employees into your home, do not pay the entire fee up-front. If someone is scheduled to come into your home, the company should be willing to tell you the name of that employee. If you want to be extra careful about who is working inside your home, ask for a driver's license and copy it down for filing in case anything turns up missing later on. You also can go outside and copy the number on the license plate of their vehicle. Don't be shy. *You* have to give that information when you cash a check. However, don't misplace something, then blame an innocent person for stealing it, possibly costing them their job. *Be certain, before you accuse.*

If you fire a home employee who had the keys to your house, change the locks immediately or have a locksmith re-order the tumblers in the locks or change alarm codes. Unless the employee is a long-serving, traditional servant, such as those employed for generations, do not grant them total access to your property. You cannot be guaranteed that the employee won't take advantage of this access, and you may never find out, until a major theft is discovered or other events reveal betrayal. You may have seen the tabloid article in 1992, sold by a man given a tour of a film star's palatial home. The snapshots of the "intruder" in the star's living room were allegedly taken by the security guard who allowed access. Sometimes, the loss of privacy is the greatest loss of all. Queens and Presidents have had employees turn on them and write tell-all books.

You must be willing to spend time to screen potential employees carefully, or you must have the money to pay a private investigator to do it. Check into childhood background, employment history, criminal history and personal finances. During your personnel interview, use techiques employed during police interviews when police are watching for subtle indicators of dishonesty in suspected criminals or potential police recruits. Watch for:

- Profuse sweating

- Lack of steady eye contact

- Frequent shifting of posture due to extreme nervousness about certain questions

- Repeated licking of the lips (fear causes tension, which often results in perspiring, thus the lack of moisture in the muceus membrane of the lips)

- Changing subjects for no apparent reason

- Evasive answers

- Nervous giggling

- Uncalled-for smirking or extreme facial movement to cover reactions to questions the interviewee may feel you would otherwise discover

- Nervous facial ticks

Allow for anticipated nervousness of anyone being scrutinized for a new job. *Trust your instincts.*

· 16 ·

Always a Weak Link,
Your Garage

The door leading from the garage into the house should be considered an exterior door. It is often one of the easiest ways for an intruder to get into your house. Too often, it is not locked. If this door is not solid-core, and you live in a high-crime area, it should be replaced, or you can add plywood to the inside of the door to further strengthen it. The interior garage door also should have a deadbolt lock. Make sure the hinges are *not* on the outside. If they are, take the door off and remount the hinges on the inside, or add a locking pin. As with any other exterior door, there should not be "play" between the door and jamb, where burglar tools could be inserted to pry the door open.

HOW TO ADD A
LOCKING PIN

Take out the screws from both hinge plates. Put in a headless screw, bolt or nail into the door jamb through the hole in the hinge plate. Leave 1/2 inch of the screw or bolt out. Drill a small hole through the opening in the opposite hinge plate. When this is completed, the pin you have added will go into the hole you drilled. The door will be held in position, even if a burglar removes the hinge pins.

The garage is a favorite entry point for home intruders. Late at night, from a bedroom or a family room, it is hard to hear someone in the garage. The garage also has tools most burglars use to burgle. If you leave your garage door unlocked or open, they won't even have to bring their own. An unlocked garage provides chances to steal cars, the contents of cars, and bicycles.

Don't buy a cheap padlock for the garage. The garage door itself should be padlocked when you are not at home. If you want to be extra careful, padlock it when you are home. Many burglaries occur during the daytime hours. If an intruder suspects the house is empty when it is not, you may have a violent episode on your hands. Minimum standard for a garage door lock: hardened steel with at least a 9/32-inch shackle. If you can afford it, buy an even stronger shackle, or purchase a five-pin tumbler with a key-retaining element. This means you cannot remove the key unless the padlock is locked. The lock, by its very design, forces you to go that extra mile to maintain security. Most combination padlocks are for high school lockers. They are usually very weak. If your padlock has the key code number on it, file it off.

GARAGE DOOR OPENERS

If you have an electric garage door opener, check the garage door once a week to make sure the door can't be lifted up. Thieves try just that, and squeeze under the door. Remember what our career criminal, "Charlie," said? Garages were her favorite entry points. And homeowners made it so easy by leaving their garage door openers *in their cars*. When "Charlie" broke into a car, she often "got a house."

A garage door that lifts can have hardened steel hasps and padlocks added to both sides of the door. Install them with carriage bolts and use large washers on the inside. After installation, some crime prevention officers recommend defacing the threads of the bolt ends with a hammer so they cannot be removed later. Weigh the work of removing them years later, during house renovation, as a small problem in comparison to fouling a home intruder desperate to get money at any price.

If you have windows in your garage, cover them. One of the first things a burglar will do is case your property; find out if breaking in is even worth the trouble and risk. He or she wants to see what you have to offer. Curtains should be drawn at all times while you are not home. They should be drawn at night, even if you are at home.

YOUR ADDRESS: ADVERTISING WHERE YOU LIVE

Don't help home intruders by giving them information they can use to hurt you. Don't put your name on your vanity license tag. Don't put your name on the mat outside your front door. Don't put your name on a small, elegant sign outside your house.

Do put your address in easy-to-read numbers on a contrasting background, for police, fire fighters, and paramedics to see in an emergency. The numbers should be at least four inches high. Have those numbers lit all night, every night. Also, paint your house numbers on the center of the driveway out by the street.

If your city or county has a police air bureau, paint the numbers on the top of your house. Las Vegas, Nevada, promoted that idea several years ago, and the air bureau police pilot, with whom we rode, relished how much easier that made his work during emergencies. If you put the numbers on the roof, which need not be visible from the street, make sure the numbers are at least two-feet high and in a contrasting color from the roof. If you live in a winter wonderland state, don't make them white. If you want to help your neighbors who cannot afford to put numbers on their roofs, use an arrow denoting the direction by which numbers increase on your street.

Hopefully, police throughout the nation will read this book, and many lives can be saved by this simple directive.

17

Vandalism and Graffiti

Times have changed. It isn't Tom Sawyer whitewashing a fence today, using his wits to dupe a pal into helping him with his chores. A lot of today's kids don't have chores. Oh, they still paint fences, but now they use spray cans. How bad can it get? One youth on the West Coast "tagged" his nickname across the country more than 10,000 times, at an estimated cost of half-a-million dollars to property owners, both public and private.

Graffiti is the most common type of vandalism. It is not always done by kids. Ex-wives and ex-husbands do it. Neighbors do it; rivals in business do it. People who don't approve of whom you sleep with, where you worship or what you believe in, do it. It's like the nuisance phone call, taken many steps further. It can be expensive; it may scare the hell out of you; but you will usually have a good guess as to who did the deed.

Officer Steve Alegre, a fifteen-year veteran of the Santa Ana Police Department in Orange County, California, has investigated complaints of vandalism ranging from shattered windows, broken automobile antennaes, deep key-scratches on cars, to toxic chemicals being dumped on gardens and lawns. Then there is arson and fire-bombing, vandalism that endangers life, scars children and often prevents families from ever making a "come-back" financially. According to Alegre, a lot of vandalism isn't petty pranks. Not anymore. Some of the most malicious vandalism is done by ex-spouses or lovers.

The city of Santa Ana covers approximately 28 square miles and has an estimated population of over 350,000 people. There are 400 sworn police officers in the police department.

The ethnic make-up of the city is primarily Hispanic, with small percentages of Caucasion, Black, Asian and Somoan. It is a perfect city for study of this subject because of city's diversity and its heavily worked and well-trained police agency.

GRAFFITI COSTS

In our travels covering the police community for two law enforcement journals, we found graffiti in small towns, on American Indian reservations, in West Coast inner-city gangs, and deep into the south. With the gang culture being glamorized in music video's, big-screen films, and Madison Avenue advertising, graffiti is exploding into all regions of our country. It brings with it severe problems for property owners. For many young people, it is their first crime, sweeping them away with a "rush" of enhanced self-esteem and power. Graffiti of any kind should be taken very seriously.

"We have two types of graffiti," Steve Alegre explains. "One is committed by a known member of a gang. Gangs now travel everywhere—Hawaii, Alaska. *Anywhere!* The other version is done by 'taggers.' A tagger's only known criminal activity is graffiti. Taggers spray their 'tag' (identification symbol) on walls, trucks, trains, everything. They are not trying to claim territory. Gangs spray their names or messages on walls to claim a neighborhood, to report what *has* taken place, or what is *going* to take place to rival gangs."

During the late Eighties, many smaller police agencies weren't aware that members of the "Crips" and the "Bloods" were travelling throughout America looking for new drug marketing territory. The tentacles spread through gangsters visiting relatives or through business intent. They would come into a small town, find the police department, and survey its resources. If everything looked weak, they set up shop. A little graffiti outside of town or scrawled on a tree or phone booth was an announcement to rival gangs that the community was already claimed.

Local law enforcement officials couldn't read the graffiti. They didn't know what it meant or who left it. Big city gang experts began making trips into Middle America, up north and down south, giving workshops on gangs and gangsters, how they operated, who they were, how to spot them, how to stop them. However, anti-gang battles were not being won in their own police jurisdications, partially because a plague was growing throughout the country and it was being ignored. There was no national coordination of effort until 1992.

How does this affect you in Nebraska or Kansas? GRATE or the *Gang Reporting, Tracking and Evaluation* system, a computer tracking system in the State of California and run by the Los Angeles County Sheriff's Department, has tracked the most vicious gang members' drug operations into every state in the Union. *Do not assume, when you see graffiti, or when you see someone scrawling or spray painting graffiti, that the vandal is harmless, or that he or she is even a local young person.* It is on record that adults who have tried to stop graffiti in progress have been shot. If graffiti goes up in your town, your police agency or city council should contact Operation Safe Streets (OSS) at 211 West Temple Street, Los Angeles, CA 90012. OSS experts will read the graffiti and analyze its message.

The Broken Window Theory

To police, getting graffiti off walls quickly is not an aesthetic pursuit. It stops crime, it stops violence. The location of graffiti has a lot to do with whether your city will remove it for you. Many cities will supply paint to a property owner, to paint over graffiti. According to Officer Alegre, graffiti that is on a non-public alley in his city, and is not visible from 25-feet of the street, is the owner's responsibility. However, the city still will supply the property owner with paint. "Once graffiti is started," Alegre says, "it is a continual problem. The average person involved is between ten and twenty years old. Primarily, they will use spray paint or heavy-duty felt-tipped marking pens. Everytime you paint over something, more graffiti goes up." Why then paint over it? Because of the "Broken Window theory."

"Where you have one block, one home or a neighborhood where things have run down," Alegre says, "where broken windows don't get repaired or where graffiti is never removed, it invites more of the same. The more vandalism and damage that goes unrepaired, the *more* it tends to increase. If a window is broken and is immediately fixed, or when graffiti is quickly painted out, the neighborhood is cleaner. It instills a sense of caring, of pride, of people staying on top of events where they live." Adherence to the 'Broken Window Theory' cuts down vandalism. Part of the growing popularity of community policing is that strong police leadership provides support for maintenance of neighborhoods. It is yet another way to fight crime.

If You Are A Victim
of Vandalism

If you are a victim of vandalism, first try to determine what the motive could be. "Often, if the homeowner has children," Alegre says, "the motive of the attacker could be the result of a dispute between a resident's children and the attacker." That is a first place to look. Do not immediately decide that the vandalism was done by a male. Girls are involved in vandalism also. If the vandalism is destruction of personal items rather than graffiti, look to an ex-lover or former spouse. If that is not an element in your life, decide who might want to seek revenge. Make a list. Sometimes it is surprising who will commit vandalism. Businessmen have been known to pay others to commit such acts. If you are a victim, be careful who you talk to about it. Your grief or terror might be just what the perpetrator wants as reward. Report the act of vandalism to police. Ask for more frequent patrols.

If You Catch A Vandal in
the Act

"Everyone has the right to protect their property," Steve Alegre says. "I would never tell a person they can't, but when a victim goes out and confronts a person in the act of committing a crime, there are risks. You don't know whether the suspect intends to do physical harm or only property damage. Maybe he wants to injure someone." When you confront a vandal, you are not only risking yourself, you may be risking your family or even your pets. The sickest vandal may attack innocent animals to send a vicious message. "Let a professional handle it," Alegre says. "Get on the telephone immediately and get the police there as soon as possible. If it is nighttime, turn on the lights. Yell from the inside that the police are on their way."

Police officers are trained to confront suspects in just such situations. "Police also have back-up if they need it," Alegre explains. "Police are armed. A private citizen may be armed, but he or she is often alone. Do not take any kind of physical force that could result in injury or death to a suspect. Legally, you do not have the right to resort to deadly force to protect property. If someone breaks your window, you cannot shoot them."

If you point a handgun at someone, you must weigh the force you are threatening against the type of crime being committed. Pointing a handgun is a threat of deadly force. "Whether it is Iowa or New York," Alegre says, "I don't know of any state that allows deadly force to prevent someone from damaging property."

MUCH CAN BE LEARNED FROM A SUCCESSFUL GRAFFITI ABATEMENT PROJECT

In the June, 1992, issue of the FBI's *Law Enforcement Bulletin*, Captain Daniel Schatz of the Los Angeles Police Department's Northest Station wrote an excellent article about police-assisted community enhancement. The article tracks the development of the Graffiti Abatement and Investigation Program. We recommend city council members and police managers read it. Probation department personnel, detectives who focus on juvenile offenders and judges cooperated in the program, making graffiti removal a condition of sentences and probations *when* community service was ordered by the courts. The abatement program is community policing at its best.

Police would identify an at-risk juvenile when his or her name appeared in graffiti or when they were caught vandalizing. Police officers would then go to the parents and ask for a voluntary parental referral to the abatement program. This was instead of charging the young person with a crime. (In such cases, police received waivers before the youth could participate in the program.)

Next, there was orientation, which included parental and offender counseling. In doing so, the officers often discovered new suspects. Vandals often travel in groups, and there are now "tagging" clubs, even in up-scale suburban neighborhoods. Sadly, gang culture is in fashion.

Paint-outs were scheduled on weekends and during non-school hours. Certain neighborhoods were targeted each time, so a solution to graffiti was quickly visible, and behavior could be more readily altered. Private businesses and community groups donated the paint, or they donated money. Professional counselors in the community donated their time. Even ex-convicts were brought into the program to counsel young offenders who thought a life of crime would be without struggle, even glamorous. Detectives kept an eye on the neighborhoods to identify areas that needed painting and to keep the restored regions under a watchful eye. An added by-product of the program was that young males became part of a work and social group, not a gang. They bonded with community leaders and good role models in the neighborhood and even formed lasting friendships with police officers. After they served their "sentences," they were allowed to continue to serve in the program for money, paid for by donations. The pay was not high, but it was a reward for hard work. Teamwork was learned, following directions, being reliable, and doing things right.

"Graffiti Guard"

If you live in a community where graffiti is an on-going problem, encourage your city leaders to look into high-tech products to protect statues, memorials, walls and the bathrooms in parks. From our interviews with police, we recommend the solution used over the 1984 Olympic murals in Los Angeles. It is called "Graffiti Guard," and it is made by Textured Coatings of America.

Clear "graffiti guard" is applied to the surface of the wall. When graffiti is scrawled onto the wall, a cleaner is applied with a rag or a brush. It's a paste-type product. After the paste is on for several minutes, the graffiti is destroyed. Tex-Coat Graffiti Guard, which was used on the Olympic murals, does not destroy the paint beneath it. In the last stage of the process, water washes the paste and graffiti off. Sound simple? Don't quit reading.

Sacrificial Graffiti Guard is a wax-type product. It is an all water-borne system. You remove Sacrificial Graffiti Guard with hot water of 180 degrees, at a high pressure. In this "system," the sacrificial coating is literally melted off. You must re-apply the Sacrificial Graffiti Guard immediately after. *You would most certainly destroy a mural with this system.* And don't forget, graffiti is put on with all types of paint or markers. Some graffiti is very difficult to remove.

Currently, an anti-graffiti coating, permanent finish, with labor, would cost around one dollar per square foot. The enhancement is, you don't have to repaint over and over. You merely clean it. With the Sacrificial Graffiti Guard, a service industry is cropping up in cities. Most people don't have power-washer equipment. Small businesses are now covering walls with graffiti guard for a price, charging a fee per month, and they come back to clean the walls once a week, for a year. As a result, the more the surface is cleaned, the less the graffiti goes up. Kids like to view their handiwork. If they know their efforts will be destroyed over and over, they will choose another wall or will tire of the whole process. An independent contractor keeps getting money for less and less work with this arrangement. But, it's usually worth it to the property owner to protect his property values and hold the line on insurance.

A warning: According to Stuart Haines, President of Textured Coatings of America, who is also on Los Angeles Mayor Tom Bradley's task force on graffiti, permanent graffiti guard is not a do-it-yourself product. It must be applied by a professional contractor. Sacrificial Graffiti Guard can be used by homeowners, but for a large surface, they will need special equipment. "In my experience," Haines said, "the majority of graffiti is on perementer walls or on commercial buildings, which you *do* have in residential neighborhoods." We suggest that homeowners' associations, ruling bodies at condominium developments and city councils gain civic involvement in this effort. The Otsey, the piece of equipment that heats water up to 180 degrees to blast away graffiti, is not something you'd keep in your garage. One more caution: With the *"blasting from hell" from the Otsey, a bad paint job or aged flaked paint will wash away.* You will have to repaint that wall.

What about toxicity? Permanent graffiti guard is urythane. It is toxic, though not much worse than paint. When you remove paint, you have the same environmental concerns. The temporary graffiti abatement product is water-borne.

If you live in a city where graffiti abounds, and you add anti-graffiti coating on your resident walls, will insurance rates go down? Yes, in most cases, but you should check with local insurance agents for actual cost decreases and what is required to qualify for them. Normally, the rate cuts are similar to those applied when you have alarm systems in your residence.

18

FENCES AND
WALLS

Fences and walls are different types of barriers: you can see through fences and they are normally built to deter the casual trespasser; walls obstruct views and are normally built to keep the determined trespasser out. In prisons, both fences *and* walls keep prisoners inside—*most* of the time. Historically, barriers have never been one-hundred percent effective. The tallest and most substantial may only deter. An example, "The Great Wall" built around 228-210 B.C. and 1,500 miles long, was built of granite, filled in with earth and reached to over twenty-feet high. The roadway on top was 13 feet wide. At about every 100 yards, it was fortified with a tower. The only man-made structure visible to astronauts orbiting earth, "The Great Wall" in China was built to keep northern barbarians at bay. It was ultimately defeated by sheer numbers of tribesmen who breached a single point.

The Berlin Wall stretched for over twenty-six miles through the capital of Germany, separating East from West Berlin, communism from democracy. Built in 1962, it was the European symbol of oppression until it fell in 1989. The wall was mined, spotlighted, patrolled by vicious dogs and sentries, and was staffed around the clock by East German border guards—"Vopos," who had orders to shoot anyone attempting to cross, either from the East *or* the West. They were not hesitant to kill. For twenty-seven years, East Germans were slaughtered or incarcerated for trying to flee to freedom. Many more thousands made it by tunneling under the wall; using deception and forged documents to pass through, they floated over it in balloons and used bribery on those sworn to defend it. One Eastern Bloc citizen even flew over it in a hang-glider.

History's lesson: barriers, even the best of them, only *discourage* penetration through accident, force or stealth. *No* barrier works one-hundred percent of the time against a person obsessed with getting over, under or through it. Human-made structures can be defeated by other human beings; if a person invented it, another person can invest like ingenuity and toil to overcome it. And so it is with security features for home or business.

Generally speaking, for walls and fences to be effective, they must be monitored either by human beings, dogs or alarms. A thief with a bolt-cutter or tin-snips can cut his way through the most expensive chain-link fence, but if the hole is detected by monitoring and reported, he will more than likely be deterred or caught. As with all security features, the homeowner or someone he or she hires must be ever vigilant. (That is one reason dogs, even family pets, are good monitors. By nature, they are vigilent about tresspassers into their and *your* territory.)

Although it depends on the degree of security you require, and the money you are willing to spend to have it, an added safeguard for enhancing the effectiveness of barriers is to light them at night. If a thief wants to breach your wall or cut through your fence, put him in the spotlight for passersby or police to see.

Finally, like The Great Wall of China, the headache of having effective barriers is maintenance. If you have a monitoring system, it also must be kept in repair. A hole in the wall is a hole in the wall, whether it was made by a crook or the neighborhood kids. A barrier to intruders is a needless expense, unless the *entire* fence or the *entire* wall is kept in good repair *all* of the time.

CONSTRUCTION

Fences and walls are constructed of the following: man-made synthetics, expanded metal, welded-wire fabric, chain-links, wood, cinderblocks, steel-reinforced concrete, and nature's own protectors such as cactus and dense shrubbery. Most homeowners associate chain-link or "hurricane" fences with security, while they look upon walls as decorative or as merely demarcations of property lines—*unless* the wall is very high. That is not necessarily true.

What looks safe and secure to a proud homeowner may look to an experienced thief like a stairway to easy wealth. In a survey of fences and walls along California's famous Pacific Coast Highway from Newport Beach to Malibu to Santa Barbara, almost every type of fence and wall protects expensive ocean-front homes. Despite their high cost, many include intimidating security gates, most of which will not keep out intruders. In some instances, the "top guard" of a hurricane fences (foot-long, steel angle-irons jutting from the fence-top at 45-degree angles that normally support several strands of barbed wire) was installed backwards, making the fence ineffective. To a security expert or anyone who has been on a military facility, such installation looks silly, yet this is the most common problem with this style of fencing.

In other cases, an impressive wall was rendered worthless by the inclusion of decorative bricks and diamond-shaped, circular or square "cut-outs." Intruders use them as peepholes for surveying the grounds before commission of a crime. Then they use them as stairsteps over the very wall intended to keep them out. Jagged, irregular brickwork serves as this type of staircase, as does natural stone.

What is the best construction material for a wall? According to architect Jeff Sulkin, steel-reinforced concrete is best. "Concrete, by itself, is not good-intentioned, that's why reinforcing is there. The second best type of security wall is dimensional stone, not a veneer, but full pieces grouted together. Sometimes there is framing behind it. It's thicker. The irregularity, the way the walls are made, makes it extremely strong.

"The problem with a brick wall," Sulkin says, "is that you have joints that line up most of the time. That's where the wall will fail. Which means, if I want to break through a wall, I chip through the joints."

What about symmetry in wall construction? "If you look at a Mayan building," Sulkin adds, "there is no symmetry. If I want to get through a brick wall, I will go right for the grout line. Natural stone walls are strong, *but if the finish is not smooth, they can provide natural ladders right over themselves.* Texture is a separate issue, but they are strong. "A stucco wall is basically hollow." It is not good for security.

WHAT CRIMINALS KNOW
ABOUT BARRIERS, THAT
YOU DON'T

Never would we compare the United States Marines to criminals, but they do have the same commitment to mission and physical skills similar to those of burglars, who are typically adventuresome males under twenty-five years old. To better understand how home intruders get over expensive, well-built barriers property owners spend fortunes to build, one need only analyze a military film made over twenty years ago. The film was a study for the establishment of standards for security barriers. That's where the Marines come in.

Five Marines were told that they could have any resource available to get over, through, or under the fences, but they couldn't cut the fences or use a truck, tractor, forklift or car to achieve their ends.

The fences included six-foot and eight-foot high, chain-link "hurricane" fences, each with top-guards of either six-strand barbed wire or concertina-roll barbed wire. (The minimum standard at the time for "hurricane" fencing, which is still minimum standard today, was nine-gauge wire strand interwoven into squares two-inches-by-two inches.) There was a maximum of three-inches of space between the bottom of the fence and the ground. At that time, razor-wire had not yet been invented. Concertina wire was barbed-wire rolled in 12-inch or 36-inch diameter "doughnuts." It is the type of barbed wire you see in movies about Vietnam and World War II.

The fence samples were approximately one-hundred feet in length and laid-out in different designs . . . parallel fences with six-feet between each fence, some with several stacks of concertina rolls, several with multiple six-strand rows of barbed wire, some with multiple top-guards and some with three parallel fence rows with concertina between each one. In one example, the Navy had piled 36-inch concertina rolls on the outside *and* the inside of a fence line. From the lay-person's point of view, no one except a highly-trained commando, with several comrades to help, could get over these barriers. In fact, some were so intimidating that it appeared an explosive-filled Bangalore Torpedo would be needed to literally blast through.

It was as good as a challenge in televised "trash sports." A game! The Marines analyzed the fence samples, then asked the

Navy for three blankets, a wood beam eight-feet long, and a large cardboard box. With these items and teamwork, they breached every fence. The average time spent was fifteen seconds to defeat each barrier, with some fences overcome in less time.

Fences are easy to defeat if the attacker is in reasonable physical condition, is not afraid to take a chance, has the time, knows what he is doing, and understands that he may get cut or deeply scratched. The Marines can do it and so can burglars. It works like this:

A Marine would run up to the eight-foot fence, stand rigid, providing a human platform for another Marine to jump onto his shoulders. The second Marine would then throw a blanket or two over the barbed-wire top-guard. He would flip himself over, lying on his stomach, then he would reach down for the first Marine, whom he would pull up and over.

If there were a large obstacle between fences, such as an open space or several concertina rolls, and the fences were closer than six or eight feet, the Marines would defeat the first fence (with the blanket and assistance-mode), and they would place the wooden beam from one fence to the other and crawl across it. More daring Marines literally ran across it. No one fell off; both fences were quickly overcome.

Obstacles between the parallel fences, like several 36-inch rolls of concertina stacked up to a height of six-feet were defeated by use of the cardboard box. The box was collapsed and doubled, thus providing strong, smooth, and light protection against barbed wire. One Marine would throw the collapsed box over the concertina and another Marine would hold the opposite side of the box, maintaining a steady, solid platform. Other Marines ran over the platform, throw the blanket over the top-guard, and then assisted each Marine over the obstacles. It didn't take long.

In some instances, if the fence was relatively simple with a small top-guard or none at all, the Marines ran up to the fence, tossed on the blanket, and shinnied over the fence with no help. Whether it be a real war or the current war on the streets, the required skills can be much the same. Part of the skills of war is not being detected until your mission is accomplished. In the case of the Marines against the fences, the barriers looked none the worse for wear. A roving security officer, unless he had a keen eye, would not have realized the fences had ever been breached.

How about injury in the process of getting into your yard or your house? As we learned in our interview with "Charlie," our delicately built, female career criminal, crooks expect to get bruised, cut and even shot. It is the cost of doing business. A little pain doesn't deter them. For many, it only makes the caper more exciting and gives something to brag about afterwards. Battle scars punctuate their war stories. They are "medals."

Defeating barriers is only an initial obstacle overcome by burglars. The bigger obstacle is hauling the stolen goods away—VCR's, TV's, pillowcases full of silverware. The loot has to be transported back over those same fences or walls. If the victim left gates unlocked, or if the gates are locked and easily opened from the *inside*, the intruder has a smooth get-away.

Fences and Walls That Criminals Like

Some fences and walls have been seemingly designed by criminals themselves. Although they are functional and pleasing to look at, or the rage of current home design, they make a house-breaker's work easy. The following is an actual survey of barriers in one square block of a small American city that has serious crime problems. Residents there have up-scale incomes, and they spend money on security up-grades. In nearly all cases, the security consulting has been extremely poor.

HOME NUMBER ONE: This house has a garage door with no apparent way into the home or attached garage. Upon closer inspection, it is obvious that a burglar could use the garbage cans, bunched together next to the garage and adjoining wooden fence, as a stepping point to a horizontal beam on the fence. He could then hoist himself onto the top of the fence. From there, it would be an easy swing to the garage roof and onto the homes's second story. (You are familiar with the phrase—"a second story man.") No one expects to be accosted on the second or third story. Most property owners have a false sense of security about that. They secure only the first floor.

HOME NUMBER TWO: Neighbors may have no concern about security. All of your good intentions and security preparation is useless if your neighbor is not as security-conscious as you are. In HOME NUMBER TWO, the resident went to great lengths to isolate his drain pipe from his second story, cutting it short, eliminating the possibility that a burglar could use it to climb above the ground floor. The quick-thinking homeowner didn't reckon with his neighbor. The neighbor built his ten-foot fence up to the property line, and added a lattice-work sun-shade. The fence and sun-shade made the perfect "jump-off" for a sure-footed prowler who would scale the drainpipe. It was a short hop to the security-conscious homeowner's second story. The ten-foot fence and sun-shade also would serve as brace and balance points for an intruder.

HOUSE NUMBER THREE: Here's another example of a burglar's best friend being an unaware neighbor. This time, the resident paid scant attention to his neighbor's ten-foot wall. The wall was superb, no foot braces, hand-holds or decorative "peepholes," but there was one problem: it butted against the neighbor's three-foot-high picket fence. The shorter fence could be used by most intruders as a stand-off point for pulling themselves up and over the higher wall. *Beware of fences and walls that abutt.*

Neighbors are not the only "friendly" threats out there. The utility companies can be awesome foes, though unaware of the dangers they may present. Utility poles for power and telephone lines are ideally suited for climbing. The experienced burglar is a natural climber, especially if it means not confronting someone on the first floor, not tripping an alarm on the first floor, or having to force entry on the first floor. People who heavily fortify the first floor of their residences, especially with sophisticated alarm systems, normally do not alarm the higher floors, nor do they keep doors and windows locked on higher floors, considering only ground floors vulnerable. It can be a costly mistake. It only takes a seconds for a burglar or rapist to shinny up a utility pole, cleave to the upper story, make his way to an unsecured door or window, and then to a victim. *Watch those poles.*

HOUSE NUMBER FOUR: There is a sturdy wood fence with heavy plastic inserts that allows sunlight to filter through the fence, while also providing privacy. You see them all the time surrounding backyard swimming pools in the Sun Belt. Really nice, until someone decides to hop over them, which isn't a great feat for anyone, from teenager to veteran crook. The sturdy trash can next to the fence only makes it easier for ANYONE to get over the fence. Trash containers should be kept inside fence lines until the morning they are to be collected—not put out the night before—and then returned to the secured area at the end of the workday, or better, as soon as they are emptied by trash collecters.

HOUSE NUMBER FIVE: This house has an unmonitored or unpatrolled chain-link fences. It does not provide a problem for any person, except against the casual trespasser or one who is trying to get large, bulky stolen articles back over the fence. One of the best home association security barrier set-ups we have seen is at the famous Malibu Colony, haven to Hollywood stars. Malibu Colony has both a stone wall *and* a hurricane fence around their beachfront compound. The two-barrier set-up is excellent, although even their wall-fence paremeter could be enhanced with top-guard on the outer chain-link fence. Design is only the first line of defense, but materials are the backbone of barriers.

Set Up for Fences

Underground support for fencing and walls is very important. Called the "flagpole condition," fence poles and walls should be built so they cannot be pushed over. A flagpole sticks in the ground far enough so that it cannot be pushed over. The earth holds it. If a flagpole were only one-foot into the ground, it might not remain erect. The same principle applies to the installation of telephone poles. Typically, a telephone pole has five to six-feet underground. Poles for a fence should be inserted into the ground following the flagpole guideline, twenty-percent or more of the total length, depending upon the make-up of the earth. Is it rocky soil? Is it sand? One will not hold like the other. Remember, if an intruder can get *one* pole to go over, the entire fence can be compromised.

Caution on Wall Set-Ups

The weakest point of a wall or building is where materials join. If you have a brick wall with a concrete foundation, the point where the two connect is the weak point. For the sake of attractiveness, do not make a wall weaker through the use of two materials, unless reinforcing is very strong.

· 19 ·

Working Dogs to
Protect Your Home

Police officers recommend dogs as among the best security alarms. Even an untrained pet can be a tremendous asset for home security because dogs are pack animals. As an accepted member of your family, a dog perceives you as being a member of his pack. Your home is his "den." He will defend you and the "den." Attack-trained dogs or guard dogs bring with their training both a keener and more reliable standard of security than the family pack-animal can give, but with their training also comes liability. In fact, since dogs are biting animals, *any* dog can be a liability for its owner.

In most states, this is how the law regarding dog bites works. If a person is on your grounds *lawfully*, or is performing work imposed upon him by law or by postal regulations, or if you invited that person to your home or grounds, you are liable for any damages your dog does to that person. Whether you have knowledge that your dog is vicious, or whether your dog has ever bitten anyone before, is irrelevant.

If your dog is there to protect property and you, and that person is on your property *illegally*, you are on stronger ground. (However, we live in a litigious society. Anyone can sue over anything.) If that person is doing something illegal in the park, which is a *public* place, and your dog bites him, you are in trouble. You may be held liable.

If you or any member of your family is afraid of dogs, and you buy a guard dog, consider that working dogs are trained to react to the "fear scent." Bear in mind, not all dog trainers believe there is actually a "fear scent."

This scent, they believe, is the sum of many factors the dog observes and detects. According to Mark Mooring, a Los Angeles Police Department K-9 specialist, they also may react to you or a family member's "fear scent." Remember, a dog does not look at the world the way you do, and a human companion must learn to see things from the dog's eyes. An example: Mooring, in his K-9 training article for *The Blue Line*, the LAPD's Protectective League publication, wrote of a police officer's severe injury, due to the dog and officer's looking at the same scene differently. If you are ever in an emergency situation during a home intrusion, Mooring's story may prepare you for what can happen when a dog is involved. The story bears repeating.

The dog "alerted" in the room, indicating he had a suspect's scent. As officers were attempting to work it out, they heard the suspect trying to exit the other side of the garage. The search team officers took up a position of advantage, which is in front of the K-9 team. One of them was crouched down for concealment.

The dog was in full alert and attempting to find the source of the scent. As he exited the garage, he keyed on the crouching officer and bit him. The handler called him off the officer, who was now on the ground. The K-9 team proceeded to the corner of the building and the handler released him with the command "find him."

Well, to the dog, this could not have been easier, since *in his mind* he had already done the right thing. He immediately ran back where he knew his "suspect" was, and the officer was bitten a second time.

Mooring cautioned anyone from trying to shoot a dog that has his teeth into someone. It is very difficult to aim properly when a dog and a human are in a scuffle. The bullets can end up killing the human.

In the incident discussed, note the injured officer was in a crouched position. That is the posture the dog would observe in a prowler or burglar. Good guys not in the line of fire might find it advantageous to stand straight, so as not to be confused with people the dog sees as enemies. Also, note that Mooring made special mention of officers getting *in front* of the dog. If you have a dog working to subdue a prowler, *stay behind the dog.*

Older Dogs

An older dog is not unlike an older person. His ability to pick up scents, to hear and to see, begins to fade as he ages. An old dog also may lack the energy required to alert you to intruders. When your working dog gets too old to be efficient, you may need another, younger one to take up the slack. A good rule is to bring in the reinforcements *before* the first dog gets too old. You don't want them to be rivals, but pals. It is more than unsettling to set the food down between two dobermans that resent each other.

An added responsibility in having a living thing for home protection is your obligation to the animal. It isn't moral to buy a dog then dump it, give it away or take it to the pound when it becomes inconvenient. Nearly all animals taken to the pound are killed, most within a matter of days. Having a guard dog is a long-term commitment. Even police dogs become pets in old age and are cared for and loved, a "thank you" for their service, and for being a member of the police family (except in the armed forces, where police dogs are inexplicably killed when their devoted services are no longer needed). Guard dogs and family pets are deserving of affection and a normal lifespan.

MAKING A HAPPY PARTNERSHIP BETWEEN PROTECTION DOG AND FAMILY

Matthew Margolis is one of the nation's most progressive dog trainers. He has excellent advice for families wanting to adopt what he calls, "The Burglar Alarm with a Heart." Margolis' training is based upon affection-oriented, positive principles. (Parents and corporate supervisors could learn a lot from him.) Dog training has been in the Dark Ages for years, primarily because it has grown from military and police work, both very conservative bastions of society. "It's Attila the Hun dog training," Margolis says. "If you read some of the old training books, you wouldn't believe some of the stuff. 'Step on his back paws. Cuff him under the chin. Grab him by the toes. Show him who's boss.' There is a better way," he says. "I've heard people say, 'I hit my kid, I hit my dog.' Would you hit a seeing eye dog, a hearing eye dog? Then why would you hit your dog?"

Police officers and military dog handlers are not prone to talk to their animals in very high, feminine sounding voices, which Margolis claims achieves remarkable results in obedience. If you decide you must have a dog for safety, consider Margolis' principles. Unlike a deadbolt lock or a firearm, a dog is not a security "object." If this chapter encourages new ownership of thousands of dogs across America, we want new dog owners to train their animals with enlightenment. The dog training style you observed in your parent's day may be considered passé in the Nineties. We visited Margolis to study his techniques. We observed him change some dog behaviors in only thirty minutes. One of his tricks: change the way *humans* behave.

"I always wondered how I would feel," Margolis said. "If I were the dog being trained, what would I want? If I were shy, and if someone taught me something, what would be the best way to learn? If I were nervous, would I want to be trained in a traffic area, or in a quiet area? If I were aggressive, is it because I'm frightened? If my trainer hits me with his hand, will I again trust that hand? (Why use the same hand that teaches, to punish?) If I am such a little dog that my owner looks like a ten-story building, why does he yell at me, when (as a dog) I hear five-times better than he does—he scares me."

Margolis does not believe in hitting, yelling or rolling up a newspaper and thrashing the dog, or kneeing a dog in the chest and screaming, "Bad dog." The secret to making a dog work for his human companions is to have his companions train him with a sensitivity to his (the dog's) personality, which can be responsive, aggressive, shy, nervous, sedate, stubborn, or a combination of those traits. Dogs are no more alike than are humans. We recommend Margolis' latest book, *I Just Got a Puppy, What Do I Do?* (Fireside by Simon and Schuster, 1992), for the enlightment of all who want to adopt a dog for better home security.

Which Dog to Choose?

Many different breeds of dogs are used as guard dogs: golden retrievers, Belgian malinois, airedales, rottweilers, and even in some cases, small breeds like dachsunds and pit bulls.

According to Los Angeles Police K-9 expert, Sergeant Donn Yarnall, the pit bull has gotten a bad rap. Yarnall claims the best dope dog he ever had was a little pit bull he got from the pound and that "he would love a person to death." Style of training or poor care, Yarnall claims, is what makes a pit bull vicious and dangerous, even to its own owner.

Should you get a small dog? A story comes to mind about the Berkeley City Council. Berkeley, California, is a fairly liberal place. They wanted a working dog, but they wanted something "short and cuddly." They didn't want an authoritative looking dog. The lieutenant who searched for such a dog griped that short dogs have a hard time sniffing out dope, especially if it's up high. "They have to be held, rifle-style," he said, "and pointed around the room." The lesson? You choose the type of dog for *your* needs.

If you want a big dog, police and security experts consider the German shepherd the most trainable. German shepherds also are adaptable to extremes in hot and cold temperatures because of their long coats. It is the German shepherd that is most often chosen for police work, partly for its public relations value. A shepherd is less offensive and doesn't look vicious to citizens, where the doberman stirs memories of a heartless police state.

It is not necessary to *buy* a good guard dog. Sergeant Donn Yarnall says that many fine dogs of working dog quality can be found at the pound. An experienced trainer can choose the right one for you.

The major crime deterrant in having a dog is they make noise. Burglary and rape are crimes of stealth. Neither burglars nor rapists want to be greeted by noise or *anything* that attracts attention. They hate dogs, and if they have to deal with one at your house, most will opt for the nice quiet home down the block.

If you want more than noise, you can match threat for threat. Many home-owners who can afford it choose an intimidating dog such as a doberman. A doberman tends to frighten most intruders, although consider that burglars don't have the values you have. Many will kill a dog for convenience.

For the more delicate owner, be advised that dobermans slobber a lot, and expensive "knick-knacks" on tables may go flying when a doberman stumbles through the room. It's a little like having your lovable Uncle Buck around the house. He may be a slob, but you've grown to like him and he's one of the family. Slight changes can be made easily to accomodate him.

How Much Will All This Cost?

A doberman puppy tested by an expert for working-dog-suitability can cost from one- to two-thousand dollars. The test is rather basic. Confidence is important. One such test has a trainer firing .22 caliber pistol shots. The puppy that runs toward the shots to see what made the sound is best-suited to be a working dog. Retrieving ability is another desired quality. Will the dog give chase? It also has to be smart. *Don't try to test a puppy yourself.* A gun firing too close to a dog may make him deaf, and he will be of little use to anyone if he can't hear. It is also uncaring. (*Do not fire a gun into the air.* Bullets must come down *somewhere.* There are *many* recorded instances where people have been killed by bullets falling from the sky, as much as from a mile away from where they were fired.)

Most law enforcement dogs are from European blood lines. European standards for the breeding of working dogs are more stringent than American standards. America focuses more on beauty at dog shows, whereas European dog shows have the Schutzhund sporting dog competitions where certain behaviors are highly sought-after qualities.

A full-grown *trained* doberman costs nearly five-thousand dollars, plus the cost of the dog. If you choose your own dog, it usually takes six weeks to train it. When training is completed at the kennels, the dog will not be an ordinary pet, nor a sporting dog. Under certain conditions, these dogs are very dangerous. That is what they are taught.

If there is an intruder, the dog often will go for the lowest point of resistance. As the intruder stoops to protect that part of his body from further painful injury, the dog then goes for the bowels or the throat. A doberman can disembowel a person. These dogs are trained to take a man *"head-on."* With this level of protection, of course, there is a price. You will need special insurance for any accidental damage the dog may inflict, for example, if the "intruder" is a utility man who has unwittingly wandered into the path of "Grinder," who is defending the gas meter from its monthly reading.

Cost for upkeep of the animal will be around three dollars a day for Science Diet, a special food orginally developed for military K-9's. Most working dog owners wouldn't dream of buying off-the-shelf dog food. Depending upon where you live, the dog will need periodic flea baths. He also will need to go to the vet for annual medical check-ups.

It will be necessary to reinforce periodically the dog's training. According to most experts, a working dog must work against a decoy or an agitator two or three times a week. If they don't, they regress and may actually enjoy an intruder's visit, showing nary a tooth. Many civilian owners won't put that much effort into maintaining the working dog's skills. If *you* don't want to face the animal in its teacherous training sessions, you may have to hire someone to do it. The dog is a valuable possession and you will not want to trust it to just anyone. It is prudent to be present during the training sessions, safely out of the way of danger, to monitor the trainer's techniques.

Working dogs trained by the most sought-after experts focus on positive reinforcement, not negative reinforcement. Catching an intruder and tearing him up, *for the dog,* is supposed to be fun. The dog is not angry, he is not upset, he is having a great, great time. The training is begun when the dog is a small puppy. A rag is used in a gentle tug-a-war.

When you see a doberman during a training session, do not be surprised at how ferocious things get. Adlercrest Kennels of Riverside, California, has a fine reputation for breeding and training world-class, Schutzen dobermans. We have studied their dogs in training. Their Schutzen dobermans will not let go of an adversary until ordered to do so. That is one of the reasons they are so prized. When Amita, who weighs in at 70 pounds, clamps onto her trainer, she will allow herself to be swung over waist-high bushes, to be covered with a blanket, to be taunted. She even refuses to chase after her coveted red ball when it is offered, *if* it means letting go of her trainer's forearm. (The trainer's arm is protected with a special, padded sleeve.) Biting the "intruder" is fun. She holds on with 2,300 foot-pounds of bite pressure per square inch. Will those powerful jaws break bones? "In a second," owner Phillip Calamia says. The "victim" or "suspect," depending upon your viewpoint, will be mangled if he gets into your house. A well-trained dog will not let go until police arrive, *or* he can hold the intruder at bay for you.

What types of behaviors can you expect from a dog like

this? If she were confronted by an intruder in her owner's house, she would sit down in front of him and bark, and bark, and bark. That is, *if* he stands still. If he moves, she will rush him and go for his forearm where she has been trained to bite. If he quits struggling, she will let go and guard him. "Most intruders, when faced with Amita, would not have the presence of mind to stand still," Calamia says. "They will struggle, and she will continue to hold on. If he fights her and tries to get away, she'll put him in the hospital."

Where do you go to find a working dog expert? There are many so-called dog "experts" throughout the United States. There are also major geographical pockets of sheer ignorance about guard and police dog training. Do not assume that all police or military dog handlers are experts. They are not. Larger cities may have the money to buy dogs for police K-9 work, where smaller towns in the state cannot. When funds are gathered to buy a K-9 for a smaller police agency, they usually choose the larger city for training, whether or not K-9 personnel there know what they are doing.

You also must consider that if you use a dog for protection or for detection of intruders, the dog may sacrifice himself for your safety. You will learn to love him, and injury or loss of the dog can be very, very painful. On your side, the best work site for your dog is *not outside*, but inside with you, where the danger to him is less.

You should also make sure your dog's training makes him "poison-proof." If he is "poison-proofed," he must take food from no one but you or a designated handler. That way, a person who wants to harm you or the dog cannot tempt the animal with a drugged or poisoned piece of steak. A well-trained working dog also is taught to behave in elevators, small aircraft and the business office. If your needs require it, check to see if he has had that training.

What type of dog should you buy? "With any breed, you get a greater demand than the quality of the supply. In other words," Mathew Margolis says, "if you look at the Sixties, there was the doberman, in the Seventies there was the shepherd. In the Eighties, it was the pit bull; the Nineties, the rotweiller. And, what do you have? We get these great movies, like *The Omen.* 'Yeah, this is the guard dog of the decade.' And, you get a lot of people in the business who shouldn't be in the business, and they're breeding without quality. If you have quality breeding, which the Germans do, you get rid of a lot of health problems."

Should you purchase a male or female guard dog? That will depend upon the individual animal. "Many people want a male because of its size. However, the female dobermans and shepherds look equally intimidating.

If you want a working dog to protect your home and grounds, it will be necessary to have high fences and well-marked signs, preferably with both drawings and wording that dangerous dogs are on the premises. Home owners who can afford it also have audio messages in several languages warning of a guard dog's presence. Be safe. Be legal. Enjoy your dog.

CARE FOR A WORKING DOG

Phillip Calamia of Adlercrest Kennel says:

On Barking: "You can control it, correct the dog, or you can do what we do when the dog hits the door. We praise it. You can buy a bark collar which gives the dog a shock when it barks. It operates on batteries. The dog will know when the collar is off, so it will bark when it should, to protect your house. Me? I take the batteries out, so Amita thinks the collar still works, but she won't get shocked. This is far more humane than cutting the vocal cords, like some people do. That has a terrible psychological affect on the animal, and a personal protection dog isn't worth much if it can't give warning."

On Fleas: "Brewer's yeast in the food or as tablets down the throat helps keep fleas off dogs. A flea infestation cannot be curtailed unless three steps are followed. The house, the yard and the dog must be de-fleaed at the same time. The dog must be given a flea bath, making sure no fleas hide inside the ears. Stuff with cotton. In California, which has a terrible flea problem, I have to do this twice a summer."

On Food: "Buy in bulk. The best food is not sold on grocery shelves. I buy 300 pounds of food at a time, a dry kibble called IAMS. I supplement it with cooked, ground chicken, enzymes for digestion, vitamin C and a pet multi-vitamin. I cook 5 pounds of the chicken at a time and mix it with five pounds of rice, with the fluid and fat drained off."

ADVICE ON THE PURCHASE
OF A WORKING DOG

PHILLIP CALAMIA

"Why is it better to buy a working dog from a European blood-line? Because in Europe, working dog competitions are like Little League in the United States. When you get that involved, you end up with the best. In Germany, breeding dobermans is very controlled. In America, breeding is a free-for-all, and show qualities are valued more than temperment or even health.

"In Germany, the doberman clubs have a breed warden. He has a lot of power. Within the first three days after puppies have been born, the breed warden makes an unannounced visit. He evaluates cleanliness and analyzes the health of both the puppies and the mother. If a breeder doesn't pass, that will be his last litter. If a dog lacks even one tooth, that dog will not be allowed to breed. Height, weight and coat are evaluated. Hips are X-rayed and evaluated for strength.

"Later, a dog fit for breeding is put through temperment tests. These safeguards are the chief reasons so many police departments go overseas to buy their animals. The dog is taken out in a field and the owner leaves. The tester walks up on the dog. The dog can sit, lie down, stand, he can play or even bark. But if his ears go down or he has signs of avoidance or fear, he fails and can't breed. In another test, they put a group of ten or more people in a line and the dog will be walked in and out of the line. The people make noise, rattle metal objects in a briefcase, for example. Someone will poke an umbrella toward the dog. Finally, the dog is surrounded and everyone stares him in the eye. That is fighting posture for an animal. This is to test his control, stability and courage.

"There is a noise sensitivity test, and finally an agitator runs from the dog and the dog must chase him and bite the sleeve. He has to take two hits with a stick without letting go. If the dog fails these tests, he can be put back for months. Or, he never may be able to be used for breeding at all. I've seen breeders brought to tears when their animals failed.

"The doberman was bred by Louis K. Dobermann in the 1890's. He was a policeman. He wanted the strength of a large dog with the tenacity of a terrior. He wanted an animal that had the *ability* to defend and protect, and he wanted a dog with the *desire* to defend and protect. The breeding of dobermans began in the United States in the Twenties, but with the beauty contest emphasis, the desired qualities of the original dobermans began to dissolve in the American blood-line. The European blood-line is carefully guarded and controlled, with all puppies' names checked and then entered in a computer—all dog shows enforced, breeding histories confirmed. There is none of this bringing a superstar into the dog show ring, allowing an unethical breeder to get a title under his name for inferior puppies, later on, from somewhere else.

"The *Dobermann Verreign* enforces that the birth of the puppies must be on the owner's property, to help ensure the owner is present to take care of problems for the mother or off-spring. It might bother some people, but if there are more than eight puppies, the others are 'put down.' There are only eight faucets, and the health of of all puppies are not risked for only a few.

"For an explosives detection dog, a police K-9 or a dog to protect you and your home, you want a stable, predictable animal that also can be a loving pet. It's too bad, but in this case I would say, don't buy American."

If You Have a Boat,

or Your Home Is

a Boat

If you own a boat, you already know that security on boats and yachts is a special problem. A million-dollar sailboat is often secured with a tiny padlock and a hasp. Motorboats, in general, have doors that close on hinges. Their hatches and windows, or portholes, close from the inside. All can be easily "jimmied." In our assessment of the inventory of a major boat equipment store, twenty-five stores in the chain all located at major marinas, we found only three models of locks being sold. They were all from the same company and all imported from Taiwan. Out of 15,000-plus articles available in each store, these were the only security items. And, the locks were not of high quality.

Boat manufacturers still, in many cases, rely on the security of a marina to protect these valued possessions. Yet, many gangways we have evaluated for security reliability are worthless in protecting either boats or people. We have easily and quickly penetrated secured areas of marinas, once getting within only a few feet of a 13-million dollar yacht, complete with its helicopter. No one asked who we were, we were never stopped, and we noted that other unauthorized visitors were on gangways, wandering around and sightseeing. Security for boats is difficult because waterways attract visitors, are often sites for restaurants and bars, and because police normally do not have probable cause to ask a potential intruder what he or she is doing there.

Will Brown is a former police officer and for years has been a supervisor in private security, managing some security operations for yacht manufacturers. Brown also holds a Coast Guard Master Certificate in Search and Rescue. He is authorized to take command of an 82-foot U.S. Coast Guard cutter, or any smaller vessel, to search for lost ships at sea. Brown has been trained on maritime crimes, piracy at sea, and stripping of stolen yachts, which often are then sunk. He says that yachtsmen themselves are responsible for much that is stolen from them.

"One fallacy yachtsmen have," Brown explains, "is that all other boatsmen can be trusted. Boating is a hobby, an interest," he says. "In so-called 'normal' society, there are socio-economic barriers. But in boating, someone who owns a small craft is almost equal in his avocation to someone who owns a yacht. When they are on the docks together, they are on a first-name basis. They tend to trust anyone who has a boat. The average boater needs to learn to be wary."

A second problem, according to Brown, is boat owners don't check on their boats often enough. "I've known boat owners who had their boats out-of-state and only spent one or two weekends a year on the boat." Who will notice? "The yacht bums," Brown says. "The people most likely to burgle or stip boats are the people who hang around, do odd jobs, 'detail' boats, or they have jobs in boat maintenance, like washing them down. They might work for a boat-towing company, they may work on the fuel dock. They will know who comes in, who goes out, who lives aboard, who does not. They will know which docks have no live-a-boards. They also have access to small boats that can approach from the water. Most thefts occur from the water."

Where does your boat hardware go after theft? Mostly, to those very boatowners who would be trusted on a first-name basis. That is the market for stolen boat parts. "They sell at swap meets," Brown says. "They put ads in the newspapers. There is a whole raft of ways to fence boat parts. For one, there is a counter-culture of people who build their own boats from scraps. They search ads for discounted items. With the troubled economy, there are also a lot of people now living on boats. In coastal cities, an older boat or a small craft is far cheaper than a house. You also have boat owners with bad drug habits. They steal expensive brass, radar units, engine parts and even dinghies to sell for drug cash."

What can the honest boatowner do for protection? Every boatowner should document his boat hardware with photographs. If police seize a garage full of stolen boat items, a boatowner cannot get his own hardware back without proof of ownership.

"A boatowner should keep his activities private, Brown says. "Don't display and don't even talk about that sophisticated navigation device you bought that will pinpoint within fifty-feet of where you are on the globe. In conversation, don't make your boat desirable as an object."

If you are going to be away from the boat, keep a light and a radio on, but use timers. If you have a hatch that is padlocked on the outside, it indicates there is no one home. That isn't going to help.

"Most burglars or strippers are going to be acting on information gleaned either from cruising the docks or from chit-chatting with boatowners," Brown says. "During that time, they are choosing what they want to steal.

Unfortunately, too many boatowners are prone to boasting about what they own. It's good to keep portholes covered so a thief can't see what you have. He may not want to spend time, or take risks to break into your boat if he isn't sure it has the items he wants."

Decals on the windows and hatches notifying passersby of security protection are a good idea, even if there is no private security back-up for those stickers. Unfortunately, special lighting is frowned upon in marinas because it disturbs neighboring boatowners.

The following is a compilation of personal protection advice for boatowners from government agencies and private security operatives. All claim that boatowners are not taking security seriously and that they are ignorant of crime prevention techniques for marinas. Here are some helpful suggestions:

- Inscribe your hull number, home port, name and driver's license number on all removable equipment, your engine, binoculars, radios, sails.

- Make a list of serial numbers and descriptions of all equipment. Take photographs. Keep these materials at home, not on the boat.

- Never leave a second set of keys aboard your boat, even if they are hidden.

- You can leave your engine inoperable while you are away. Or, remove the rotor.

- You can drain the fuel. Install a secret cut-off switch.

- Put special transom bolts on outboard motors.

- Start a Neighborhood Watch—"Marina Watch."

- Moor your boat to something secure. Make it so the cable can't be lifted over.

- Use one-way bolts, backup plates and lock nuts.

- Run a cable around and under a thwart (or stanchion).

- Make sure all hinges are on the inside.

- Put auxilliary locks on the insides of portholes.

- If your hasps are not inverted, replace them. Use only the strongest padlocks.

- If thefts are occurring in your area, lobby for better lighting of the piers and barriers to the piers. Too many barriers are just for show. They can be climbed or jumped over, thwarted in numerous ways. According to Will Brown, security gates on most gangways are "horribly designed." The best are "large, with metal rods and gates, with barbed wire, and are canted. Gravity closes the gates."

   A CAUTION: Compare shop for security items and proper installation. Let only an expert handle your boat security needs. If installation is not done correctly, it can affect the re-sale value of your boat.

· 21 ·

Safe Rooms

Be it a controversial politician afraid of the cruelist of enemies, a film star tense about obsessive fans, a divorcee fearful of a vindictive former spouse, or simply a homeowner who wants to feel a little more secure about his family while he is out of town, a Safe Room can provide the ultimate in personal security. To analyze the most elaborate designs in Safe Rooms, one need only focus on those historical figures who created the most extreme of enemies.

Hitler created his safe haven at Obersalzberg, a mountain-top hide-away where he took retreats. Called "The Eagle's Nest," it is one of the most elaborate Safe Areas ever built. In a most dispicable move by the Nazis, a total of twenty-seven farms and private homes were seized in 1936 and 1937 to provide Der Fueher with this beautiful and very safe place. Amusing, in terms of today's gated communities, a visitor had to pass through three gate houses staffed with armed guards on the way up the mountain.

Hitler's large complex was underground. In Goering's section, as described by Josef Geiss in his book about Obersalzberg, Geiss states the safe area had "3 meter-thick walls of iron concrete. A thirty- to sixty-centimeter-thick concrete lining was fastened to the walls which was covered with cement . . . and was insulated by some kind of roofing felt or artificial rubber tilt. The insulation was protected by a twenty-five-centimeter thick wall. Ground water was conducted to the canalization through built-in trickle stones in the concrete lining. Thick iron plates and other safety precautions were adjusted to the entrances . . ."

"Did this underground safe area look like a bunker? Not from the inside. In Hitler's Safe Rooms, architects used wood wainscoting, rugs, marble, and included beautiful dressing cabinets and an inlaid floor. A straight corridor up to the entrance offered covered safety of 30 to 50 meters. Sub-tunnels carried technical systems such as ventilation equipment and electrical cables. Hitler even had a special room for his wolf-dog. Eva Braun, his mistress, insisted on her own bathroom, and Bormann wanted his own dining room. Bormann confiscated other areas for storage of silver, jewelry, thirty-six tailer-made suits and his books. There was such an excessive amount of preparation in Bormann's "safe rooms" that experts claim he could have lived there for 200 years. ("The ordinary people," according to Geiss, "employees and workers, about 1,000, had to be satisfied with only 385 square meters of underground space." *Their* tunnels were muddy and had benches. And not enough benches, indeed.)

In the summer of 1992, Americans were surprised to learn that in the event of attack, Washington's lawmakers were to have been housed in a lovely underground complex, equally secure as the Congressional rotunda, not far from Washington DC. Safe Rooms have existed throughout history, be it a section of a cave with a secret exit, or today's Safe Rooms in Beverly Hills' mansions.

Safe Rooms are not unobtainable for the average homeowner. They are not difficult to incorporate into an existing home. You may not be able to afford a vault where your whole family can live comfortably for weeks, but a closet for storing valuables while you are away on vacation is not out-of-reach.

Jeff Sulkin, one of our experts on security design, discusses bullet-proof glass: "It's expensive. In one of my projects, it was tested in a real-life situation. People always ask about it, and most of the time, they don't want to pay for it." According to Sulkin, the people who most often request bullet-proof glass feel exposed. If they have a ten-by-ten foot window in their front room, they understandably feel they are being observed. "I try not to have those windows facing the street, or I put a tree in front of it, or have an overhang. Whatever gives the quality of not being exposed."

However, if a client must have bullet proof glass, the cost goes up 10 percent per square foot. "It's astronomically expensive," Sulkin says. "And it's very, very heavy. There is laminated security glass with layers of mylar or kevlar between the layers of glass. There is a material known as Nomax. If Kevlar is manufactured in fine mesh, you can see through it."

For a Safe Room, there should be no windows, or extremely small windows made affordably secure. The most common perception is that Safe Rooms should be in the basement, but Sulkin, who has designed them, disagrees.

"If there is an intruder, and you are home, it will probably be at night. Pick a space that is near the bedroom, because nighttime is the time you'll most likely be surprised and unprotected. Then you can have a floating piece of metal plate in the walls, or use Nomax panels. Kevlar, from which they make police bullet proof vests and military helmets, is light and strong. A Kevlar layer behind the plaster will stop bullets or an ax."

The Kevlar panels cost between six and eight hundred dollars for a five-by-ten-foot sheet. The cost doesn't come with buying the Kevlar itself. It comes with having a builder work with this special material. A specialized carpenter will be needed. There may have to be conferences between contractors and the Kevlar company about special glue or special considerations about temperatures and installation. "In construction," Sulkin says, "you pay for having someone working with it. What the builder will charge to install it will reflect his discomfort and unfamiliarty in using it. He doesn't do it everyday. There are builders who work with it a lot, but they are the most expensive builders."

Should a Safe Room be on the ground floor? One theory is that intruders can get to you faster if you are on a ground level. "Look for a space near the bedroom," Sulkin advises. "A place that doesn't have a lot of windows. A walk-in closet doesn't have a lot of windows. The closet becomes the Safe Room." There is a trend in residential design to have a roof hatch or hidden doors out of buildings—a way out. If you worry about being trapped in your home by an intruder or enemy, consider that secret way out.

Another of our experts, architect Edward Carson Beall, recalled a client whose daughter had been raped. Beall designed a secret staircase out of the daughter's bedroom closet, an escape that made her sleep easier after her cruel experience. Sulkin designed a fake heating grill in one up-scale home that was actually a hatch to flee the house.

"If regular burglars get into your house," Sulkin says, "they will look under the floor and behind paintings for your safe. A safe can go into the Safe Room, not in the bedroom. In terms of the ultimate Safe Room, consider a walk-in closet and a bathroom connected. In there, you already have a sink, a toilet, a shower, and often furniture. It works." The floor and ceiling should be of concrete or Kevlar.

When building or remodeling for security, frequently there can be an aesthetic conflict. Do you really want a concrete building? Do you want your doors made of metal? There are doors today that are grained to look like wood. And one of the nice things about thermal glass is if there is a fire, it can't get through thermal glass as quickly as regular glass, which pops out from the extreme heat. A glass door that is double-glazed will last longer during such an emergency because the heat differential is taken up with the dead air space.

Sulkin suggests a fire-rated door. "The client may tell me, 'I'm willing to have half my house burn down, but not while I'm sleeping, not where my kids are, not where my safe is and not where I keep my valuables.' So we put in a fire-rated door, commercially rated, with a steel frame, with a double-locking weather gasket, which is like flashing. Theoretically, that will stop a fire for one hour, two hours or three hours, depending on the rating."

Can you be compromised by your construction crew, familiar with your efforts to protect family and treasures? Of course. That is why Sulkin advises that safes and tunnels never be included in building plans. *Ever.* "What you say is, 'I need these beams six-feet apart.' You never say, 'Put the safe here.' You just leave the space. Toward the end of the project, you cut a hole in the plywood when the majority of the workmen are no longer there. It's good to do it on a weekend."

An escape tunnel? Who digs the tunnel? "Dig the tunnel for another reason," Sulkin says. It's an 'access tunnel.' Put a pipe in it. It's an access for future electrical lines. If it's oversized, say they want to get into the cracks."

When you deal with sensitive security upgrades or security design, should you pay more to the workers who perform those tasks for you? The answer is no. "It piques their interest," Sulkin says. "They start to think." In construction work, the final toil is performed by skilled contractors. The pouring of concrete and putting up studs is done by unskilled labor for the most part. Don't do the security work until those laborers are gone. Not that unskilled workers are less honest than skilled ones; it's that such a plan takes one layer of employees out of the picture prior to security work.

Certified Protection Professional Tom Conley stresses that a Safe Room have a cellular telephone in it. A cellular phone is always a good back-up for an alarm because if the phone lines are cut, you still have communication capability with the outside. "It is also important that a cellular phone be checked monthly," Conley says. "And you need to get on the monthly rate scale. You can get a cellular phone for fifty to sixty dollars a month in many states, and the calls are only fifteen-cents. Or, you can get one for twenty dollars a month, and the calls are a dollar. You won't be using the cellular phone a lot. It is a security item, so choose the rate scale where each call is a dollar with that lower monthly fee. It's an emergency phone."

Conley also says the home's alarm system panel should be located in the Safe Room, and the locks should be controlled from inside. Other necessary items are: fire extinguisher, blankets, water and food. Weapons? It depends on whom you consult. "I would have a large caliber revolver," Conley says. "I would definitely have a weapon in there. Probably a .357 magnum. A 9mm would be even better, but the problem is, people buy their gun and they never learn how to use it. When an emergency arises, they can't figure out how to get the magazine in. 'What does the little red dot mean?' The thing with revolvers is that they are fairly idiot proof." The down side of a revolver is with some people under extreme stress, manual dexterity and fine movement goes away. When you are upset, trying to get a bullet into a little hole can be *very* difficult.

Jerry Wright, a Certified Protection Professional headquartered in Anne Arbor, Michigan, recommends a solid wooden or better yet, a metal door for a Safe Room. The door should have reinforced framing and it also should be fire resistent. "You want to limit the knowledge of others that you even have a Safe Room," Wright says. "Don't brag about it. Don't tell people. If you have weapons, store them there. Items you need for ready access, jewelry, papers, can also be stored in the Safe Room, things that wouldn't fit into your safe deposit box." And don't forget the kittie litter.

· 22 ·

Safes

Safes serve a variety of purposes, from protecting valuable papers from fire and theft to storing firearms and large amounts of cash. In some embassies overseas, as well as super-secret government agencies and think-tanks, the final bastion of safety for agency and diplomatic personnel is a huge safe, containing communications equipment, arms and ammunition, a recirculated air supply, food and water, and personal comfort items. Safes are versatile and expensive.

Architect Edward Carson Beall, who designs homes located in some of the most expensive cities in America, recently added a vault to a master suite in a multi-million dollar home. The vault was to protect a family of four in case of burglary or home intrusion. It has a self-contained breathing system and water. The vault, Beall said, was similar to a bank vault, proving that if you can afford it, you can give the crooks some snappy surprises.

According to our police sources on both the East Coast and West Coast, more middle-income people are buying safes. This is because of the lowered interest rates and distrust of banks and Savings and Loan businesses. Immigrants, many of whom come from countries where citizens trust neither banks nor police, also are keeping their money at home. Home intruders know the score. They are now looking for safes.

To put a floor safe into an existing home, a hole is made in a concrete slab. The cost of making a "setting" for the safe will depend on where you live. In large cities, the cost for setting the safe runs around one-hundred-and-twenty-five dollars and up.

A good contractor can have it done in half an hour. Customers rarely install safes themselves, unless they have a slab ready for it. A square is framed out prior to having the concrete slab poured, and the safe goes in later.

Because of the design, technology, and materials inherent in modern safes, the cost can range from one-hundred to ten-thousand dollars for a safe installed in a home. The minimum you would want to spend for a good safe would be around two-hundred-and-fifty dollars. A used safe from a "tear-down" may cost less. In Nebraska or anywhere outside the Southern California area, you might pay more. The reason—Southern California is the core of the safe market. Horizon, Star Major and other safes are manufactured there.

One manufacturer, Gardall Safe Corporation (1-800-722-7233), issues a lifetime replacement assurance on all its safes. This corporation also makes products ranging from 462 cubic-inch wall safes to 37,000 cubic-inch gun safes. Gardall also builds custom safes, especially for clients who require cladding, encasement, snorkles, chutes, drop slots, or rotary hoppers. If this sounds confusing, it is meant to be, since you must consult a professional safe manufacturer to find out what these terms mean and if they can be useful to you. Gardall offers a Group II electronic lock option, which has, among other things, a six-digit push button combination, one-million possible combinations, easy combination change from the key pad, and a device that activates a lock-out delay when someone enters four incorrect combination sequences. Again, the advice of a certified locksmith is desireable for complete and correct information on safes.

On fire-rated safes, the industry and UL (Underwriters Laboratory) minimum standard is the capability of protecting papers for one hour at a maximum external temperature of 1,700 degrees Farenheit. That's enough heat to melt brass. This means that papers in a test safe during the one-hour heat test remained pliable and legible because the inside temperature did not exceed 350 degrees Farenheit, the charring temperature for most papers. Should you purchase a fire safe, ensure that this minimum standard is maintained. A good, small fire safe, about two cubic feet and weighing over one-hundred pounds that is manipulation-resistent and adheres to UL standards should cost, at a minimum, about two-hundred dollars. Again, compare, shop and read *all* the details of sales materials.

A fire-rated safe is different than a floor safe. A floor safe is made of solid steel. The door should be a minimum of one-half inch steel, the bottom should be one-quarter inch, and you can get heavier from there. The fire safe, on the other hand, is like a tin can full of insulation—sheet metal and insulation with locking bolts. If someone were to pound on it, they could get into it fairly easily. It is hard to get both elements together—fire safe with attack-resistence. For that, you're looking at two-thousand-five-hundred dollars and up. (For composite safes, one-half inch steel door, one-quarter inch steel body.) The customer has to spend more for fire-rating. Made of concrete and formicalite, it will hold moisture. If you're protecting diskettes, you can't have that moisture. You'd need a different type of safe altogether. You'd need a safe *within* a safe. AMSEC makes them (home office in Fontana, California.)

What about the difference between a half-inch steel door and an inch-thick steel door? According to one safe expert, "If you have a half-inch thick door, you'll get a thug pounding on it for four days to get into it. An inch-thick door, he'll pound on it for six days. Professionals who will drill it out or manipulate it, won't take more than five minutes. So, if you're worried about four or six days of pounding, you have a problem." The lock expert selected for HOME SAFE HOME, Tom Vessels, claims that if he were going out to open your safe because you lost your combination, it would take him, on the average, two minutes to get into it. Does he use sounding devices like the safe-crackers on TV? The only reason he'd wear them is for concentration, *not* to hear the tumblers fall. "Only TV does it that way," he said.

Vessels shares a good story about safes: "There's this guy who owned a pawn shop. He had this big safe and it was specially made. A great big, tall thing. Big old wheels on it, all kinds of levers and gears. Two dials on it. And, he'd had probably thirty break-ins and nobody ever got into that safe. That safe was nothing but a big steel box. That's all it was, with all those dials and gears on it. If the burglars would have looked on the wooden floor, they would have seen the tracks where the guy rolled the safe forward. The whole back was open. He'd take out what he needed and pushed it back to the wall. Fifty percent of the battle is where the safe is hidden. I know people who have a floor safe, and they went out and bought a cheap little fire safe and put it in the closet. Just set it there. When they got broken into, the fire safe was found quickly, but the floor safe was never disturbed. It saves a lot of abuse on the house."

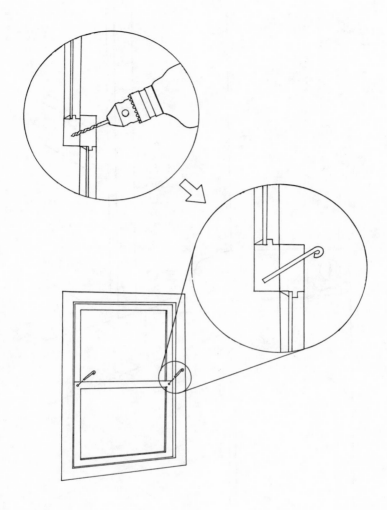

By drilling an angled hole into both parts of the window frame, a screw or bolt can be inserted to restrict the movement of both windows. The angle ensures that the screw or bolt is not shaken out.

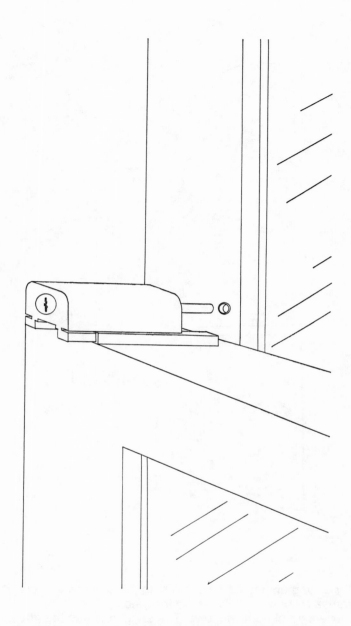

A common window latch that requires a key to lock or unlock it. Although not as popular as the thumb latch, which operates on the same principle but does not require a key, this latch is extremely effective at stopping intruders from covertly opening the window.

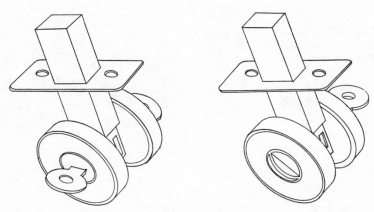

Two deadbolt locks. At the top is a thumb turn, at the bottom is a double-cylinder lock that requires a key to unlock both sides. Both deadbolt locks have a one-inch "throw," the end of the bolt that protrudes into the "strike," the plate mounted on the door jamb. The double-cylinder lock is preferred for total home security since a burglar cannot exit the home through the door, precluding him from carrying large items from your house.

Remember, not all graffiti is done by local kids. Some serves as a warning to rival gangs that the territory already has been claimed.

The top fence has a topguard, or outrigger, that faces the direction of attack, and the fence goes all the way to the ground.

The topguards on the bottom fence face inward, making the act of scaling this fence easier, and the chain-link does not extend to ground level.

The fence poles, or spikes, of the top fence, plus the points on the carriage light, are intimidating and probably will make an intruder think twice about trying to scale it. The intruder, however, will not think twice about suing the fence's owner if he is injured trying to get over it.

The bottom fence, although not as intimidating, will most likely stop the casual trespasser, which is all fences like these are designed to do. The bottom fence also will keep the owner from spending many hours and dollars in court.

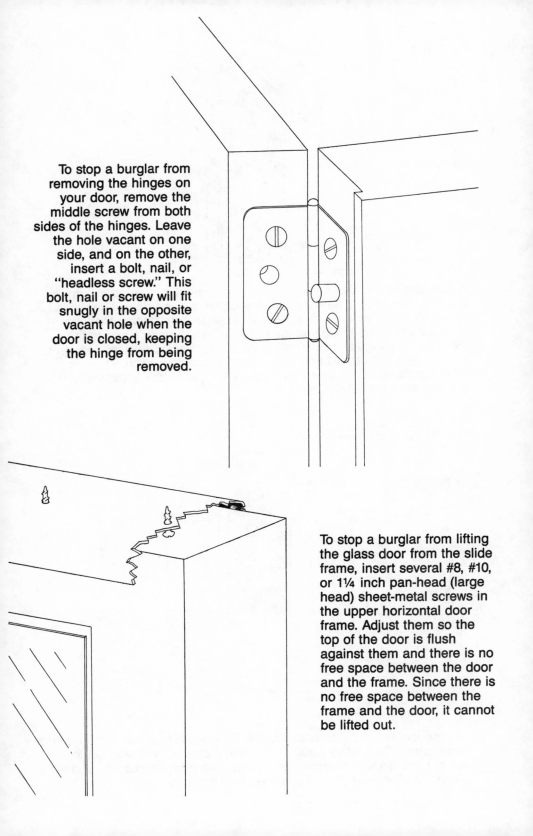

To stop a burglar from removing the hinges on your door, remove the middle screw from both sides of the hinges. Leave the hole vacant on one side, and on the other, insert a bolt, nail, or "headless screw." This bolt, nail or screw will fit snugly in the opposite vacant hole when the door is closed, keeping the hinge from being removed.

To stop a burglar from lifting the glass door from the slide frame, insert several #8, #10, or 1¼ inch pan-head (large head) sheet-metal screws in the upper horizontal door frame. Adjust them so the top of the door is flush against them and there is no free space between the door and the frame. Since there is no free space between the frame and the door, it cannot be lifted out.

A beautiful, expensive door that also is designed to provide maximum security. The door is heavy wood, the frame is wood deeply imbedded in concrete, and the decorative glass silhouettes surrounding the inner door are stout and small enough not to allow a burglar's arm to fit through. The large door also is set back into the doorway far enough to prohibit an outstretched arm from reaching the door latch. There is ample lighting for the door and alcove provided by the small watchman lanterns on each side of the door.

A security-oriented entranceway. The door is solid and set back into the door frame. Decorative glass in the door frame is small enough to restrict access to the interior door latch. The exterior walkway and the interior alcove are lighted by indirect wall lanterns.

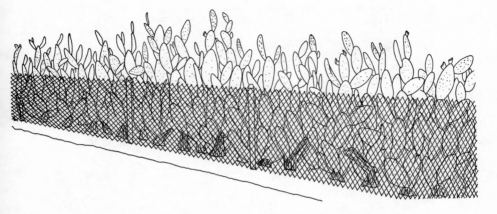

Vegetation, as well as steel and wood, makes effective barriers. In this case, an experienced burglar probably would rather attempt to get over the chain-link fence than crawl through the cactus wall. Use vegetation as a security barrier when you combine protection measures with aesthetics.

This greenery is undoubtedly keeping the summer sun from roasting the residents of this home. It is also the perfect hiding place for a burglar, peeping Tom, or rapist to plot a crime and "case" the premises. Keep shrubbery, trees, and bushes cut back from windows and doors, and keep the bottom of such greenery trimmed high so that a trespasser's feet and legs can be easily seen.

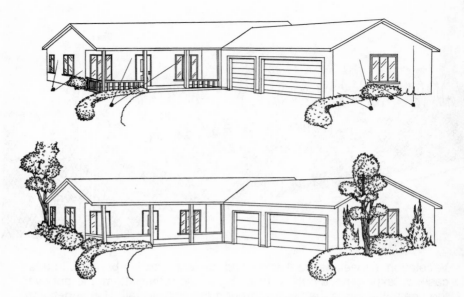

The top house is well-illuminated with offset lighting, trees and shrubs have been cut back from the sides of the home, no trees lead to the roof, and a trespasser can be seen easily through the porch railings. The bottom home has no illumination, a thief can hide behind the low walls of the front porch, and shrubs and trees can protect a crook from being seen by passing police.

Beware of decorative glass in doors.

Focus on Youth

Every security program in which a family is involved should include the children. It is important to discuss security with children, to keep them involved in the changes in security procedures or the operation of home equipment, and to solicit their input about what security means to them and how they can protect themselves and feel safe. However, unless family security involves extreme circumstances, it is inadvisable to alarm children or make them paranoid about society's dangers.

AVOIDING VICTIMIZATION

Children should be told how to avoid becoming a victim. The National Center for Missing and Exploited Children (NCMEC) of Arlington, Virginia, is a private non-profit organization established in 1984. It works in conjunction with the U.S. Department of Justice in coordinating the efforts of law enforcement, social service agencies, judges, and the public and private sectors to break the cycle of violence that historically has perpetuated crimes against children. The NCMEC advises the following for the protection of children. The age-old rule of teaching children to stay away from strangers creates a false sense of security, for child and parent alike.

Sadly, it is often a family member, friend of the family, or a neighbor who abducts, molests, or murders a child. According to experts at NCMEC, the term "stranger" suggests a concept that young children often do not understand, and it is one that ignores what we know about those who usually commit crimes against children. Sometimes children are misled into believing that they should beware *only* of a person who has an unusual or slovenly appearance. Instead, it is more appropriate to teach children to be on the lookout for certain kinds of situations or behaviors rather than certain types of people.

Children can be reared to be polite and friendly, but it is good for them to be suspicious of adults asking for help. Children help other children, but there is no need for them to be assisting adults. A ploy used by child abductors is to ask a young person to help them find a lost kitten or puppy.

Children should not be asked to keep "special secrets" from their parents. Children should not be asked to touch anyone in the "bathing suit areas" of their body or allow anyone to touch them in those areas. A child should be taught that the moment someone insists on a "special secret" they are to keep from their parents, they are to tell their parents immediately.

Often exploiters or abductors initiate a seemingly innocent contact with the child victim. They may try to get to know the child, to "befriend" them. They use subtle approaches that both children and their parents should be aware of. They often will look for victims who are in need of attention or love. Children from broken homes are high-risk.

Children should be taught to stay away from people in cars and vans. They also should be taught that it is alright to say NO—even to an adult. They should not be drawn close to a vehicle where they can be dragged inside. Further, the NCMEC has some tips for parents about preventing child exploitation:

- Know where your children are at all times. Be familiar with their friends and daily activities.

- Be sensitive to changes in your children's behavior; they are a signal that you should sit down and talk to your children about what caused the changes.

- Be alert to a teenager or adult who is paying an unusual amount of attention to your children or giving them inappropriate or expensive gifts.

- Teach your children to trust their own feelings, and assure them that they have the right to say NO to what they sense is wrong.

- Listen carefully to your children's fears, and be supportive in all your discussions with them.

- Teach your children that no one should approach them or touch them in a way that makes them uncomfortable. If someone does, they should tell a trusted adult or their parents immediately.

NCMEC instructions for children include:

- If you are in a public place and you are separated from your parents, don't wander around looking for them. Go to a checkout counter, the security officer, or the lost and found desk and tell the person in charge that you are lost and need help.

- You should not get into a car or go anywhere with any person unless your parents have told you that it is ok.

- If someone follows you on foot or in a car, stay away from that person, even if it is a woman. You don't need to get near a car to talk to someone inside. Keep your distance from the car, even if the person says you must come close because he can't hear you. That is a trick.

- Grownups or teenagers who need help should not be asking children for help; they should be asking older people. Don't be fooled by this request.

- No one should be asking you for directions, or to look for a "lost puppy," or telling you that your father or mother is in trouble and that he or she will take you to them. Get away, get help and find a trusted adult.

- If someone tries to take you somewhere, quickly get away from him or her. Yell or scream, "This man is trying to take me away" or "This person is not my father (or mother)."

- You should try to use the "buddy system," and never go anywhere alone.

- Always ask your parent's permission to leave the yard or play area or to go into someone's home.

- Never hitchhike or try to get a ride home with anyone unless your parents have told you that it is OK to ride with him or her.

- No one should ask you to keep a special secret. If he or she does, tell your teacher or parents immediately.

- If someone wants to take your picture, tell him or her *No*. Tell your parents or teacher immediately.

Don't be fooled into thinking that all molesters are "strangers" or "dirty old men in trench coats." Don't think that all people who molest children are homosexual, mentally disabled, lurking in alleys, parks, or schoolyards, or addicted to drugs or alcohol. Some "strangers" are tall and handsome, well-dressed, educated, and very personable. Some can be extremely convincing to children, parents, teachers, and even police. However, children should be told not to speak to strangers, not to get into stranger's cars, and not to take presents, especially food, from strangers.

Since adults are physically stronger than children and easily can drag a small person into a car, children should be told to sit down immediately if anyone tries to force them into a car or van. They should not voluntarily enter the vehicle, help the adult get them into the car, or assist in any manner whatsoever. The child should begin screaming loudly for parents, and keep screaming for them, until a parent, a teacher, or a police officer responds. This will accomplish two things of vital importance: ideally, it will prevent a kidnapping by scaring the kidnapper or molester away. If nothing else, it will cause such a commotion that passersby or neighbors will be attracted to the scene and will be able to take immediate action. If the suspicious adult is not apprehended, then adults attracted to the scene will be able to get identifying information for the police, such as the suspect's description, description of the suspect vehicle, etc. Immediate notification of the incident and a complete description of the suspect and his vehicle to the police will have dramatic results and may prevent a horrible tragedy.

Personal alarm devices for children have been advertised on television and radio. One such alarm was tested by a nationally syndicated consumer advocate show. A child with this device was placed in a crowded mall and instructed to use it.

The child activated the alarm. The only thing it caused were angry and irritated stares from passing adults. No one came to the child's rescue, stopped to ask if there was a problem, or even stopped to tell the child to stop making the racket. Obviously, this product didn't bring about the advertised result. As an adult, ask yourself, What would my reaction be to a certain alarm activated by a child? Your answer will dictate the type of alarm you may want your child to carry.

Suggestions for a child's personal alarm device extend from crude, loud police whistles to a fist-sized, compressed-air alarm called, appropriately enough, "The Screamer." This device is carried by thousands of women across the nation as a deterrent against muggers and rapists. These simple devices will attract attention, but all have one problem: they must be activated by hand. They are not self-activating upon an attempted theft, kidnapping, or molesting; thus, they are worthless in locating a lost or errant child who does not want to be found.

Some of the more successful personal security devices that are ideal for young people include a keychain alarm that emits a shrill 105 decibel alarm, a compressed air cartridge, pocket siren that shrieks at 140 decibels, and a smaller pocket alarm that hits a would-be abductor with 90 decibels of shocking sound and can't be turned off without removing the batteries. Most alarms like these sell for less than twenty dollars, are activated by simply pressing a button or switch, and run either on batteries or compressed air. They are child's play to operate.

CURIOSITY KILLS

During the Fifties, a major concern of parents across the United States was the chance that young children, while playing in back yards and vacant lots, would be accidentally suffocated in abandoned refrigerators and freezers. This concern led to legislation, with stiff penalties, that barred discarding refrigerators and similar appliances that had working locks, hinges, and hasps. Today, this hazard has been virtually eliminated by strict enforcement of the ban. However, locking devices, and in some cases their absence, still present a danger to small children.

All drugs, firearms, and cleaning substances MUST be hidden or locked away from children. Children have no concept of danger, especially in their own homes, and are trusting to the point of death. A simple padlock and hasp arrangement is sufficient, keeping in mind that the key to this lock must be SECURED or HIDDEN out of sight *and* the reach of smaller hands.

Refrigerators and freezers, used daily or on a regular basis, must be kept closed and secured. The refrigerator in the kitchen is not normally a threat since it is usually full and cannot accomodate a small person who wants to crawl inside. However, many families keep a refrigerator or freezer on the patio, in the basement, or on the service porch. It is these containers that are a hazard since sometimes they are empty or near-empty and can be opened by small, prying hands. They provide a crawl-space, nice and cool on a hot summer day, for a tyke who has no idea of the deadly threat. Screams from inside cannot be heard. These, too, should be fitted with a hasp, and a padlock placed and locked.

Calling for Help

Children should know who to call for help if they are involved in an emergency or are going to be late returning home. For very young children, a laminated index card, with a few names and telephone numbers of trusted adults, should be carried at all times, preferably secured in some way to their clothing. It is important that this card be laminated because younger children tend to spill things on themselves and their clothing, and the chances are great of spilled liquids causing the letters to run on the card, making them illegible. Lamination sheets usually cost less than a dollar at a stationary store. Large retail outlets sell them from coin-operated machines.

In the event that a person exists whom parents DO NOT WANT CALLED for help, this name, without the telephone number, should also appear on the laminated card, along with specific instructions that this person NOT BE CALLED. This precludes a well-meaning adult from calling someone the child knows only as "Uncle Bernie," who lives on so-and-so street, and whose telephone number could be found easily in the local phone directory. If "Uncle Bernie" is drunk every night, you don't want him driving your child home.

Ensure that your child knows how to operate a telephone, even if it only means that he or she lifts the receiver, dials 911 or

Operator, then talks to the voice on the other end. For smaller children, this could mean how to lift a telephone from the cradle (pay phones included), how to insert the quarter that is in a safety-pinned pocket, or always attached to a shirt, how to dial 911 or a memorized number, and what to say.

Babysitters

Horror stories abound about "killer babysitters" and those who rent themselves as overnight nannies in order to be alone with young children for less-than-honorable purposes. A recent motion picture, *The Hand That Rocks The Cradle*, described the horrible ramifications of making the wrong choice of nannies; the same can be said of making the wrong choice of babysitters. Just as it is baffling that corporate executives will entrust their entire business to after-hours, inexperienced guards with unknown backgrounds who work for minimum wage; just as shocking is that every day and every evening, caring parents entrust their children to inexperienced babysitters with unknown backgrounds who work for minimum wage. Just as baffling is the horrified reaction of caring parents when they are confronted with the fact that their child has been severely injured or killed by a person they never should have trusted in the first place.

Conduct a background investigation of the person you entrust with your children. It can take the form of a single interview with the potential "sitter," or a documented, in-depth inquiry by a qualified background investigator. Excellent choices for this task are retired police officers who become licensed private investigators.

In the background investigation, a list of questions should include the following:

1. Is the person of sufficient age to handle my child and the problems associated with children, to the standard I require? Is the person, because of his or her age, liable to invite friends over while I am away, putting his or her personal desires above the welfare of my child?

2. Is the person of sufficient maturity to be left in charge of my house, and everything in it, and my child? Can she take care of difficulties, make the right decisions, quickly notify the right people (such as the police and fire departments), and take the right action to protect my child and my household from danger? Is the person level-headed and not prone to making STUPID decisions?

3. Does the person know First Aid and CPR? Can he or she treat a small cut, administer the taking of required pills, or staunch severe bleeding in the time it takes for medical professionals to arrive? Will the person panic at the sight of blood or a serious injury?

4. Has the person sufficient experience in watching small children, or is this the first time, and is the child the "guinea pig?" Can the person supply references from other parents who will attest to her maturity, caring ways, and proper supervisorial traits?

5. Does the person have an arrest or criminal record? Although it is generally illegal to base denial of employment upon an arrest record alone, it is prudent to determine if the person to whom you are entrusting your child has ever been arrested for child endangering, physical abuse, narcotics or drug usage, burglary, theft, sex crime offenses, or any other crime that could be perpetrated in your home, against your child, in your absence. In a small town, the local police may help you in this regard, but in large cities and metropolitan sprawls, the police do not normally conduct background checks in these matters. A security consultant or private investigator, for a fee ranging from one-hundred to five-hundred dollars, usually will conduct an extensive background investigation, which may include past acquaintances, criminal history, employment history (including reasons for termination or resignation), credit status, and other items for which you express a concern.

Although these signs may indicate problems other than sexual abuse, physicians warn that the following common physical signs may be indicative of sexual molestation:

• Sexually transmitted diseases.

• Discomfort in the genital area (bruises, swelling, bleeding, fluid discharge).

• Stained or torn underwear.

- Frequent headaches or stomach aches.

- Pregnancy.

- Difficulty walking (especially if the child is very young).

- Difficulty in male teacher's classes, excellence in female teacher's class (as a pattern, not individual class).

A CHILD'S VIEWPOINT OF
SECURITY HARDWARE

At a minimum, the two locking devices that young people must know how to operate are the deadbolt lock and the standard doorknob lock. Show the youngster how they operate and what each lock does in each position (locked and unlocked). If necessary, especially for younger children, paint instructions on the deadbolt lock or on the door, just opposite the lock, such as red and green arrows, the red meaning "locked." The green means "unlocked." For doorknob locks, paint the button in the doorknob center red, and instruct your child to, "push the red button ONCE to lock the door, and push it TWICE to unlock it. Turn the knob this way (whichever way retracts the bolt), and open the door." Make it as easy as possible for your child to keep bad people out and to escape from the clutches of bad people if they are inside your home. Give the kids a quick way out.

If you have a key-operated, interior deadbolt (double cylinder deadbolt), make sure your children know the EXACT location of the key to this lock, and make sure THEY CAN GET TO IT, QUICKLY. Make sure they know it is alright to use this key, that daddy or mommy won't scold or punish them for using it if they use it when they are allowed to. Don't confuse them with a bunch of difficult or convoluted events that would or would not permit them to use the key. Just tell them that if it is an emergency, and they have to get outside quickly, USE THE KEY; explain to Daddy or Mommy later why the key had to be used.

Instruct your children that if they must get out of the house during an emergency, especially during a fire, to open the door or break a window, BUT GET OUT OF THE HOUSE. Make sure they know that if it is an emergency, that someone is trying to get them, or that there is a fire in the house, they are to *GET OUT OF THE HOUSE.* After the situation has been resolved, the parents can talk to the children about how they exited the residence.

Practice drills, including an easily identified rally point outside the danger area (across the street by the big elm tree, over by Mr. Wilson's mailbox, etc.), where "noses will be counted," is one of the best ways to ensure children do not panic during an emergency. This is especially true if you live in a home with more than one floor or story.

The important thing about security and children is awareness and how things work. If a child understands how to open a door by unlocking the deadbolt, or what a prohibited situation is, or when he or she may be in trouble with a stranger, their chances of surviving are tremendously enhanced. What you don't teach them leaves them vulnerable.

WHEN THEY ARE
HOME ALONE . . .

Intruders may not always leave your home alone just because they find the front door locked. Some will smash the door to gain entry, especially if they know that no adults are home; most brazen burglars and petty thieves are not afraid of children, even large teenagers. In riot situations, such as those occurring in Los Angeles, Atlanta, and other cities in May 1992, it may be necessary to counter the "kick-ins." Emergency barricading is useful and may save the life of a child left alone during civil unrest.

Most chairs cannot stand the impact of a determined "kick in" and should not be counted on to support the door. Since most young children do not have the physical strength to move a couch or heavy piece of furniture across or against the door, how is the home defended? Thinking back to old movies, the good guy would jam a strong, stiff-backed wooden chair against the doorknob and the floor, making it near-impossible for the bad guys to break into his room or office. This method works, to a certain degree, but can be defeated in time by a large man, continually and doggedly, throwing his weight against the door.

What is needed here is a light tool made to do what the

strong, stiff-backed wooden chair did for the movie hero. A product called "The Jammer" literally is supposed to jam a door so that it must be destroyed to come down. Made of durable aluminum, it telescopes from 25' to 42' and can be jammed under a doorknob to keep the door intact under repeated kicks or can be placed in the frame of sliding glass doors to keep them from being opened. It can be used easily by children, with instructions from adults, and sells for under twenty dollars.

Children normally are not as resourceful as the young hero in *Home Alone*, and in the average American residence, there are not nearly the tools and items used in the movie to dispell the two bungling burglars. However, there are some things you can teach your children when it comes to home security.

Tell your children never to open the door to strangers, no matter what he or she says or how convicing they may be. Some typical ploys used by crooks against younger children include:

"Your mommy told me to check on you, to see if you are alright. Please open the door, just a crack, so I can see you, and tell her that you are OK."

"I have to deliver this package to your dad. If I leave it out here, he will be very angry and spank you when he gets home. Now, open the door and take this package . . . or, I'll just slide it inside, and your dad won't be mad."

"I'm a policeman (or policewoman) and you better let me in. If you don't you'll be in trouble, and I'll arrest your mommy when she comes home. Now, you don't want me to do that, do you?"

"I have a special present for you from the toy store. Your mommy said I could give it to you. Now, open the door and take your surprise."

Installing a peephole in exterior doors is a wonderful idea, but peepholes for adults are usually installed at eye-level, much too high for a child. Have a second peephole drilled at the eye-level of your smallest child, so that they, too, can see who is at the door.

Install peepholes at lower levels in bathroom and closet doors, wherever you have instructed your children to hide in case of disturbance or intrusion. Naturally, these doors should have interior locks, but a peephole, especially at their level, provides additional insurance against them being victimized in their own homes.

SEXUAL EXPLOITATION

Child molesting is often a repeat crime, and many kids are victimized over and over, often by the same person. The reality of sexual exploitation is that the child often is confused and unwilling to talk about the experience to parents, teachers, or anyone else. But THEY WILL TALK if you have already established a feeling of trust, support, and love in your home, whereby your child will talk without fear of blame, guilt, or accusation.

Parents should be alert to indicators of sexual abuse. According to experts in crimes against children, common behavioral signs are:

- Acting out inappropriate sexual behaviors or showing an unusual interest in sex.

- Bedwetting, nightmares, fear of going to bed, or other sleep disturbances.

- A sudden acting out of aggressive or rebellious behavior.

- Changes in behavior, extreme mood swings, withdrawal, fearfulness, excessive, unexplained crying, and clinging to parents.

- A fear of certain places, people, or activities, especially of being alone with certain people. Children should not be forced to give affection to an adult or teenager if they do not want to. A desire to avoid giving this affection may indicate something is amiss.

- Acting younger than he or she is. Regression to infantile behavior.

- Poor schoolwork, frequent absences.

- Shame about his or her body.

- Loss of self-respect.

WHAT TO DO IF YOUR
CHILD IS MISSING

Parents frequently expect the worst when they can't find their child. Visions of injury or kidnapping flash through their minds. The mother is usually the one to make the discovery that her toddler is no longer in the backyard. Upon making this discovery, she makes a hurried check of the neighborhood, calling for the child. If she finds the child, all is well.

The case where the child is not found in only a few minutes is the one that causes parents and police anxiety. Let it be said, however, that there are very few missing children who are not found in a few hours.

If the parents were to do the following things, missing children could be located easier and sooner.

- Remember that all children wander at some time or another. Therefore, you should check on them regularly.

- If you do not locate your missing child within a *short time*, notify your local law enforcement agency at once. The sooner police are on the job, the easier it is for them to locate the youngster. Time is important because young children sometimes wander great distances from their homes in a short period of time.

- As a parent, you can assist a great deal if you will enlist your neighbors and the older children of the vicinity in the search. These people know the child and can spot him or her from a distance, while police officers are working from a physical description.

- Keep someone in the home of the missing child, preferably the mother. The child may return, and if no one else is home, he may wander away again.

- When checking the neighborhood, check *every* house and backyard. Don't skip around. Very often, missing children are found in nearby homes.

- If it is evening, and both parents are home, one of the parents, preferably the father, should join the neighborhood search. Don't do as some people do—just sit around or go to bed and wait for the police to find the child. Assist them in any way you can.

- Be sure to check every room in your home. Check *in* and *under* the beds. Look *behind* the furniture. Look *under* the house, in the *garage, chicken house,* or *other out buildings.* Young children often crawl in these places and then go to sleep.

- Stop and think about what the child has expressed a desire of doing or wanting or seeing. This may prove a valuable clue about his location or destination.

- If you locate the child and you are the person who reported him missing, notify the police at once. Many times in the past, police officers have continued the search long after the child was found by parents. It is a waste of community resources.

- It is important to remember this: If a young child comes to *your* home, and he or she normally does not visit you, contact the child's parents or the police. He may be a missing child for whom the neighborhood and police are searching. Many times police officers have had to work all night in search of a missing child who was already asleep in bed with friends because the people with whom he was staying felt it unnecessary to notify parents until the following morning.

24

Pets That Flee During a Burglary

Cameron White worried about what would happen to her pets if her home were broken into. Burglars, when they flee, frequently do not close a window or a door, especially if it is the back door, out of sight of passers-by. Dogs and cats get out, and while wandering, can even be stolen.

Also, if a burglar is within a home, and the police arrive, they may not realize that sounds coming from a darkened bedroom may be a pet walking around, not the burglar. Pets can be shot.

White came up with Pet Alert, a door hanger to be hung on the *inside* knobs of exterior doors. She wanted it to be affordable for the elderly. It retails for less than ten-dollars. The door hangers are large and brightly colored enough (only certain colors are easily visible through smoke) for firefighters to see them through protective masks or thick smoke. Pet Alert was designed with the help of both police agencies and firefighters.

The door hanger contains the following information: pets by name, type/breed, color and location if the pet is caged (a bird or reptile). The hanger includes your work telephone number, an emergency number, a relative's phone number, a veterinarian's phone number.

Pet Alert comes with an outside sticker that contains no private information, but the outside sticker is good for security in two ways. It may deter a burglar who doesn't want to take his chances with whatever type of animal is in your home; he won't know by looking at the outside sticker. It also allows police or firefighters who have to enter your home to grab the door hanger once inside and prepare themselves for handling your pet, or saving it. Police officers have been sued for killing a pet during a search. A security measure such as this can prevent tragedy for officers, the animals and pet owners alike.

25

Television Monitoring Systems

Homeowners who have a lot to loose, be it either material possessions or personal safety, may need to monitor their grounds and home twenty-four hours a day. Since hiring three or four private security guards to walk the grounds may be too expensive, the next best thing is a television monitoring system. Situations where a security designed television monitoring system may be helpful include:

- Where the house is too large or the yard and land surrounding it is too vast to monitor without the help of modern technology.

- Where the need for privacy is paramount and the resident wishes to remain concealed while monitoring visitors.

- Where there may be a threat of personal injury or theft of property and the resident wants a record of who visited the premises during a specified period of time.

- When there is a need or desire to monitor several different directions or sections of the grounds or home at one time, as thieves, vandals or visitors move from one place to another.

- When a resident is too frail or is unwilling to leave the safety or comfort of the home to find out who is on the grounds, or if he or she if fearful of "buzzing" someone in without having more than a voice upon which to make that decision.

Basically, two television monitoring systems are available, each with numerous features of varying sophistication. Since most residents rely on security consultants who work for the very companies that install the systems, the average home owner often pays far more than is required for adequate equipment. First, there is the system where all cameras are linked to one television monitor, which has a switching system. Second, there is the system where each camera has its own monitor. Obviously, the second system is the most expensive. Industry often uses both systems. Even the most expensive home would not require both systems, unless the homeowner is unusually paranoid or has the resources of an aerospace company.

The advantage of having the multiple monitoring system is that it is much easier to track a moving burglar. If the intruder moves fast, and most do, it can be difficult to follow him as he does his dirty work. If there is more than one intruder, as with home invasions by Asian gangmembers, multiple cameras allow all villains to be tracked and recorded. It's great evidence for use in court later.

It doesn't make much difference if you have the most expensive, elaborate monitoring system money can buy if it is not used properly. If you are fortunate enough to have a security operative within your grounds, as many celebrities and company executives do, then realize that watching monitors causes security guards to go blank after many hours at this boring duty assignment. Actually, the single monitor can keep them more alert, because they have to *do* something . . . push that button and make selections of what to look at next. Another rule—a security guard, be it for a gated community, a condominium complex or for a home, should not be reading or watching commercial television, even listening to the radio, while on the job. Take newspapers and magazines away. Television security equipment is only as effective as the person hired to watch it. We have observed the following infractions: a guard lying on the floor of a darkened sentry booth watching commercial television, a guard away from her post in the restroom doing her hair and applying the day's make-up, and a guard masturbating while thefts were in progress, visible on his nearby television monitor. Monitor the person who monitors your system.

PLACEMENT OF EQUIPMENT

Important when selecting a television monitoring system is how they function in dim light and what the environment is like where they will be mounted. If you own a million-dollar beach house next to a public access-way to the shoreline and there isn't much light on that long wall at midnight, you have two choices. You can brightly light the entire wall every night for a year, which will cost you big bucks, *or* you can illuminate only enough to deter burglars and *then* buy an expensive light-sensitive camera. A light-sensitive or "low-light" camera works like the aviation goggles military pilots wear during night combat. Existing light is intensified so the pilot can identify what he or she needs to see. The same goes for a security camera. You only need what is required. Find a balance between light and camera so that you or your security employee can identify what you *need* to identify. If you only want to spot a body going over a high wall, you don't need the highest priced camera or the brightest light.

The effect of environment on this type of security system is also crucial. Whether you live on the slopes in Aspen, in the extreme heat of Palm Springs or you've retired to the steamy delta of the South, the extremes of hot, cold and humidity need to be considered if you want a television security system to be effective and to last.

Thanks to NASA and its efforts in miniaturization for the space probes, security lenses are now so small they can look like flies on a wall. If you've been in an expensive hotel lately, your face is probably on video tape. The lens can be peeking out of a plant, from the face of a clock, or through that wonderful mirror you used to adjust your tie. It could be concealed almost anywhere. Not all television security cameras are obtrusive. In fine hotels and in the homes of top police executives and corporate presidents, there is an effort to make guests comfortable in spite of security observation. No one wants to feel like he or she is constantly being observed. Unfortunately, in today's society you often are. On the plus side of concealment is the fact that when the camera is concealed with only the lens visible, the camera also can be housed for environmental protection.

Depending upon the system you buy, consult first with a veteran television technician or a Certified Protection Professional about where you want the cameras to be located, their scope and what protections against the environment will be needed. A word to the wise: When the camera itself is concealed, but the tiny lens is not, make sure the painters don't paint over it. Also, keep it free of cobwebs.

Finally, there are homeowners who use cameras for "monitoring," when they actually have no such system hooked up. The cameras themselves often deter misdeeds. Whether the cameras work on an actual electronic security system or not, they have to look serious. In mounting your cameras, make sure they are high. If someone can reach up and drape something over the lens, they will look useless to the professional criminal. They will not deter him.

Many security vendors refuse to quote prices without sending a sales person to your home. They claim that if they quote basic prices, competitors will immediately "low-ball" them in this very competitive business.

One technique for making a quick sale is to quote an inflated price, to "high-ball" customers, telling them that if they sign "today," the cost will be hundreds or even thousands of dollars less than that quoted price. Don't sign. Get quotes from several companies, regardless of how troublesome it may be to go through multiple security assessments. It will be worth it.

Burglar Alarms

The term "burglar alarm," even though widely accepted, is a poor designation for such a device simply because these alarms detect other things besides burglars, such as *any* person or animal entering the area being protected by the alarm. A limitation of alarms is that they only notify a person or monitoring station that an intruder has penetrated a building or its grounds. They do not physically keep people out. Alarms cannot protect. Do not allow alarms to give you a false sense of security. They malfunction, and response of police or private security personnel may be slow. Alarms only harden a target.

Residential burglar alarms can be purchased from most electrical and hardware dealers. Alarm companies sell or lease entire alarm systems. Before purchasing or leasing an alarm system, homeowners should check with their local police to determine if their community regulates security consultants, alarm companies, alarm installation and monitoring, or alarm sales practices. If there is a state law or city ordinance, check to see if your alarm sales person or installer is in compliance.

If you install your own alarm and are not a professional alarm installer or an electrician, most probably you will install an audible alarm, one that emits a loud noise from a bell, a tone generator, or a siren. The sound of an audible alarm going off is an excellent deterrent to an amateur burglar. However, for an audible alarm to be effective, neighbors hearing it must call the police. It is important for you to notify your neighbors that you have installed an audible alarm. Test it in their presence so they know what it sounds like. Make sure it can be heard by the neighbors. Request that, should they hear the alarm go off when you are not at home, they immediately call the police.

Ideally, a burglar alarm system will have a failsafe battery back-up, and a readout ability that tells you if the system is working or not. It is recommended that you do not have an auto-dialer system installed that automatically calls the local police. This may seem self-defeating, since you want the police notified if an intruder tries to break into your home. The *ideal* alarm and notification system is monitored by human beings, and the decision to call the local police is made by a person, not a machine that mindlessly dials, redials, and redials. Avoid auto-dialer systems, especially if you live in an area susceptible to natural disasters, such as earthquakes, tornadoes, hurricanes, and floods, for an auto-dialer will completely block incoming phone calls to the local police agency during such a crisis.

WHAT ALARMS ARE
SUPPOSED TO DO

Normally, burglar alarms make immediate notification if an intruder is trying to enter a protected space or has been successful in entering. An intruder's presence in a protected space, such as your living room or your yard, is detected by a sensor, which then triggers the alarm, making notification to either the police, the subscriber (homeowner), or the local alarm monitoring company. Based on location, sensors are usually divided into three categories: point of entry (door, window, etc.); an area of protection (back yard, living room, etc.); and point protection (an object, such as safe, desk, computer, etc.).

To account for all happenings, sensors should be capable of signaling an alarm under any of the following conditions: an intrusion or attempted intrusion into the protected area; unauthorized opening of the housing that encases the sensor; grounding, shorting-out, or disturbance of the alarm system circuitry; power failure; and failure of the sensor itself, due to aging or lack of maintenance that renders it ineffective. Additionally, sensors for indoor use should be able to operate in temperatures of 32 degrees F to 120 degrees F, while sensors located outdoors, or in structures without heat, should be capable of operating in temperatures of minus 30 degrees F to 150 degrees F. Notwithstanding these requirements, sensors should always be operable at 90 degrees F and a minimum of ninety-five percent humidity. By and large, the type of alarm you have is not as important as the type of sensor(s) you have.

SENSORS AND WHAT
THEY DO

It may seem needlessly technical for the average home-owner, but knowledge is power in the world of sales. Know what you are buying or leasing. Learn the language of the alarm business.

There are many types of sensors in use today and in any number of configurations, combinations, and categories. Sensors range from the standard electro-mechanical devices that react to interruption of an electrical current to the sophisticated thermal-sensitive devices that actuate an alarm if body heat is detected.

Electro-Mechanical Sensors

Electro-mechanical sensors provide reliable service, operate on basic principles, and are simple to install. They are primarily used to protect openings, such as doors and windows. Because they are simply designed, they may be defeated by a knowledgeable burglar. These sensors contain conductors that carry electrical current, which maintains an open position in a holding relay. If the current is disturbed by the opening of a window or door (breaking contact), or if the current is cut off, the holding relay closes and an alarm circuit is activated. There are many types of electro-mechanical sensors in many forms— pressure mats, foil, contact switches, and screen and wire detectors. Each is tailored to a specific use, but generally they are designed to protect entry-points.

Foil is normally used to protect glass, either in windows or doors. It comes in one-half-inch or one-inch widths and is placed around the visible, outer edges of windows and other glass panes. Foil applications usually can be seen in jewelry stores, some banks, and businesses, safeguarding precious metals or large amounts of money. The principle behind foil application is simple: foil conducts electricity. When the alarm is armed (placed into action by the homeowner), the foil conducts electricity from one end to the other, forming a continual, unbroken circuit. If the foil is broken, and it is fragile, the circuit is broken and an alarm sounds. Foil is a thin, metallic tape that should not exceed 1.2 pounds tensile strength. It should be able to carry a maximum electrical current of 60 milliamperes at 60 volts, with a maximum temperature rise of one-degree centigrade. For proper conduction and to reduce the risk of tampering, foil should be installed on the interior of the protected surface. Characteristics and drawbacks of foil include: it can be seen easily in its normal installation and can be defeated by a professional burglar. Since it can be seen easily, it provides a psychological deterrent, discouraging most undetermined amateurs. Application of foil is not easy and requires an experienced installer, but the cost of foil itself is inexpensive. Being fragile, foil is subject to breaks and the ensuing false alarms caused by these breaks. Breaks in foil are common, caused by temperature and humidity-induced tape expansion and contraction and accidental and intentional scratches.

Contact switches are routinely used to protect openings such as doors, skylights, and windows. Based on a simple design of continuing electrical current, the sensor is composed of two electrical contacts. One is installed on the opening surface (the moveable window, a moveable door) and the other is installed on the fixed surface (the window frame or door jamb). When the window or door is closed, the two contacts are face-to-face together. A continual electrical current is maintained between the two contacts, as long as the opening surface and the fixed surface are together. If the opening and fixed surfaces separate, the current flow is interrupted and the sensor triggers the alarm.

Contact switches may be magnetic or mechanical and may be either surface mounted or recessed into the protected fixture. To avoid intentional or accidental manipulation or compromise of contact switches, they always should be installed on the inside of protected areas. Naturally, surface mounted switches can be seen and are less expensive than recessed switches, which cannot be seen after installation.

Contact switches normally are installed in positions that allow for slight openings or tolerances, thus avoiding false alarms. Slight gaps should be planned to compensate for minor play in opening surfaces, but no more than two-inches.

Of all the intrusion (contact) switches, the most effective is the balanced magnetic type. This sensor announces an alarm when the magnetic field is increased, decreased, or a substitution of an external magnetic field is attempted. To ensure the best working capacity, the following two precautions should be taken by installers: the gap between faces of the switch housing and the magnet should be adjusted to accomodate installation variances; and the switch should be electrically protected against voltage surge.

Screen and wire sensors are made of fine, hard-drawn breakwire to construct grids, screens, or lacings on building surfaces or openings. These screens, grids, and lacings are capable of supporting electrical current. If any part of the hard-drawn wire is cut, grounded, broken, spread, or nominally disturbed, the alarm is triggered. This sensor is programmed to react to a spread of wires more than 96 square inches, the size of a manhole.

The composition of screen and wire sensors should be solid copper, hard-drawn, and not larger than Number 24 Awg (American wire gauge). They also may be enameled solid copper wire, not larger than Number 26 Awg, or the equivalent. Wire and screen must be capable of carrying an electrical current of 60 milliamperes at 60 volts, with a maximum temperature rise of one-degree centigrade. Tensile strength of this wire and screen should not exceed four pounds.

Fences may incorporate wire sensors. A single wire may be threaded along a fence or wall and set to notify an alarm if the tension on the wire is disturbed by anyone attempting to climb into your protected area.

Prefabricated sensor screens also are available. A screen of this sort should be installed in such a position that if any portion of the screen is moved more than two-inches away from its attached surface, an alarm is activated.

Unless you have money to burn, don't buy wire lacing. Another type of sensor should be used to protect these floors, walls, ceilings, etc., at a fraction of the cost of wire lacing.

Pressure mats are used to protect entranceways, stairs, or certain areas of carpeted space. Normal weight restriction for activating these alarms is from five to twenty-pounds. It is usually resistant to most damaging elements, but moisture may erode the wire and connectors. This threat to trouble-free operation may be eliminated by sealing the wire and connector in epoxy. Be informed of such details when talking to a security consultant or alarm installer.

Vibration Sensors

Vibration sensors are nothing more than small, extremely sensitive, contact microphones installed against or inside walls. (They may be used on other surfaces.) Usually ineffective outdoors, they are keenly effective indoors and detect the minute sounds of a burglar attempting to penetrate a wall or enter the area. The sensor is adjusted to eliminate the sounds that are normally present in the protected area. However, penetration sounds such as ripping, chiseling, jimmying, or cutting, are detected and transmitted to an amplifier. An alarm is then activated.

Good locations for vibration sensors are on the inside surfaces of vaults, inside walls, on floors, on windows, in ceilings, or directly on filing cabinets, desks, computers, or safes. They are well suited for reinforced walls or masonry.

Sound Wave and Microwave Sensors

These devices operate on the principle that microwaves and sound waves are disturbed by movement and that disturbance can trigger alarms. Soundwave sensors are commonly referred to as ultrasonic detectors because they use sound waves of a higher frequency than humans can hear. Microwave sensors emit electronic waves, but on a much lower spectrum, like a microwave oven.

Their operation is based upon the Doppler principle, the same principle that is used in radar and sonar. Sound waves and microwaves are generated out in a certain direction, like a shotgun. These waves bounce back from any obstacle. The pattern in which the waves bounce back is "read" by another sensor, and a pattern is made from it. This pattern is then compared with other patterns kept in storage. If the discovered pattern is new, an alarm sounds. For instance, if a sensor's computer has stored patterns of tables, corners, chairs, desks, and other known objects in a room, and waves "bounced back," it indicates the pattern of something not previously identified in the room—such as a person. Soundwave sensors are best suited for indoors, while microwave sensors are more effective out-doors.

Microwave sensors also have been called radar detectors because these sensors and radar both operate with microwaves. Microwaves sent forth are reflected back to an antennae, which then sends the reflected patterns to a comparison circuit. If the comparison indicates no change in the microwave, all is well. However, if a moving object has changed the microwave patterns, the comparison circuit will activate an alarm. Used inside a room, it floods the space with microwaves, similar to the flooding of a space by soundwaves. Used outside, the microwaves are generated in a small beam to a receiver or antennae in a straight line along the perimeter of a protected area. Good things about the microwave sensor include: they are generally unaffected by air movement, temperature extremes, atmospheric disturbances, or noise; and they are good for outdoor use and do not falsely alarm in rain, snow, heavy fog, or sleet. Some bad things about microwaves are: they can be interrupted or intercepted by metal objects, so any movement behind items made of metal will go undetected; and they can penetrate walls made of common materials, such as plaster and cement blocks, which makes for false alarms when the sensors detect movement beyond these walls, outside the protected area.

Ultrasonic sensors have some draw-backs. They have a range limit, so it may be necessary to use more than one in a large area. Also, what is in the area, or how a room is constructed, will affect the performance of the ultrasonic sensor. Rooms without furniture affect soundwaves less than rooms filled with sound-absorbing furniture, carpets, and drapes. Since an ultrasonic sensor is not affected by exterior noise in the audio range (it reacts only to movement within a protected area), it does not cause false alarms because of movement beyond the walls of this area. However, air currents can cause false alarms in ultrasonic sensors, so air movement generated by air conditioners should be considered. Ultrasonic sensors detect *any* movement.

Some areas covered by ultrasonic sensors also use an alarm discriminator, a device designed into the sensor to eliminate certain movements, patterns and noises. The discriminator filters certain items so that the sensor does not sound an alarm when it detects them, such as birds, animals, the vibration of an airplane passing overhead, etc.

Audio Sensors

Audio sensors, which can receive soundwaves, consist of microphones, which can be hidden inside a room. An amplifier receives disruptive sounds and triggers an alarm. Some intercom systems can be modified to act as audio sensors. Outside sounds can trigger an audio sensor and cause a false alarm. A sound discriminator should be installed to filter out unwarranted noises from the amplifier.

Capacitance Sensors

These devices operate on the principle of detecting something that absorbs energy. A capacitance sensor is a large electric condenser that gives out energy and senses change in the capacitive coupling between the ground and an antennae. Anything that absorbs energy near the sensor, such as a person or animal, will produce a disruption in the balance between the ground and the antennae, causing the sensor to activate an alarm.

The capacitance sensor works poorly outdoors because atmospheric changes cause the capacitance levels to change and activate false alarms. Best suited for indoor application, especially large areas, they are easy and inexpensive to install. Vibrations and noise do not disturb capacitance sensors.

Light Sensors

Light sensors operate on the principle of disruption or interruption of a projected light beam causing activation of an alarm. A change in the light level also will cause an alarm. If an intruder alters the pre-set light level, either by a flashlight or by turning on the lights, a light sensor detects this change and activates an alarm. Since the light sensor has a photoelectric cell to determine light levels, and since most photoelectric cells react to both visible light and invisible light (infrared), it is possible to place an infrared filter over the light source, making the light beam invisible. In this infrared mode, light sensors have been called "beam sensors" and "invisible eyes." In a non-infrared mode, where the light can be seen, the most common use of this sensor is as an entranceway alarm, where a person entering or leaving interrupts the light beam and sounds a buzzer or bell.

Passive infrared motion detectors operate similarly to light sensors, only they detect changes in the pattern of thermal energy in a protected space. It is known as "passive" because it emits no energy or light source, relying upon an optical system that projects an image of the protected area, or object to be protected, onto a radiation sensor. The radiation sensor registers the amount of thermal energy and establishes a pattern of thermal energy in the space. Movement by an intruder changes this pattern and activates an alarm.

Light sensors work well outdoors *and* indoors. Outdoor use requires that the sending unit be protected against the weather; individual heaters assure a constant operating temperature. Mirrors can be used to alter the projected light path around corners or objects, although reflection weakens light strength. Lasers have been used in light sensor applications. A laser beam is an enhanced light signal. It can deliver an extended range between a transmitter and a receiver. Lasers are generally less expensive than normal photoelectric detectors.

Other sensors used mostly in commercial applications, although available to the homeowner who can pay, include balanced pressure sensors for outdoor area and perimeter protection, thermal sensors that detect body heat of an intruder, a chemical sensor that detects human effluvia in the air and sounds the alarm, and a radiation detector that senses human presence through radiation principles. In the latter, no danger exists, due to the extremely small amount of radiation used in the sensor. It is not a popular sensor because consumers associate the word "radiation" with danger. Even closed-circuit television can be modified to detect a change of televised pattern in a protected area, thus activating an alarm.

If you have a large home to protect, it is recommended that a combination of sensors be installed and monitored. In this way, the deficiencies of one sensor that might cause a false alarm can be compensated by another alarm. A simple "check and balance" system is preferred over standardization of sensors in any large area to be protected.

If you want a burglar alarm system and not just a single, audible alarm, it is best to purchase or lease an entire system from a licensed, reputable alarm dealer. This can include alarm monitoring services. Most dealers sell both burglar and fire alarms. They can incorporate the best intruder sensors with the best smoke and flame detectors. If you are a renter, before you can have an alarm system installed, you must have the written permission of your landlord.

Ask a minimum of three alarm companies to inspect your home for its security weaknesses. It is not foolish to do this. We have found that architects often learn their security design skills from interviewing security sales people. One prominent architect said he'd interviewed eight sales representatives for the security aspects of only one house.

Security inspections of your home should be done separately, with no two sales representatives there at one time. Sales representatives are business competitors, and they may "low ball" their cost estimate only to come back later after you have awarded them the contract with "new discoveries" about your home and the security system that will cost you extra. Security company sales people should be punctual, courteous, reasonably groomed, and well-informed about the alarm installation and security business in your area. A thorough security inspection, including discussion, suggestions, and comments, should take no more than one to one and one-half hours. Study this chapter before you have your security inspections so that you can better ask questions.

Request a written security plan to protect your home. After you receive several written recommendations, compare them against one another for price, service, warranty, credibility, and credentials of the owner *and employees.*

The following items are critical regarding a home security inspection. Make sure that the alarm company representatives includes them on their company letterhead:

1. Full name and telephone number of the representative inspecting your home and making the estimate;

2. List of access points (door, window, French doors, skylight, etc.) where the representative recommends having a sensor installed, the type of sensor suggested, and the reasons *why* each sensor should be installed at that access point;

3. The price. For a two-bedroom, 2,000 square-foot home, the average cost runs from $450 to over $1,800 for purchased equipment. This price must include the difference between *leasing* the sensors and equipment and *buying* the sensors and equipment;

4. The annual price for monitoring service. Across the United States, the monthly fee for alarm monitoring is between 20 and 35 dollars, depending upon location. If a recommendation is subscription to an alarm monitoring service, get an answer to the following questions:

1. Is the central monitoring station UL (Underwriters Laboratory) approved? If not, why not?

2. Is the monitoring station local? If not, exactly where is it (some stations are *several* states and thousands of miles away from the subscriber), and who will monitor *your* account (human or machine?). Does the remote monitoring station rely upon toll-free (800) telephone numbers to receive alarm notifications? (In the past, a popular long-distance telephone company lost several series of (800) alarm-response numbers during a high-alarm period.)

3. How long is the monitoring service contract? Why? (The ideal term is one year.)

What is the false-alarm rate on the type of sensors the company representative recommends? What is the false-alarm rate for the company? To verify this answer, check with your local police crime prevention officer, who may have false-alarm statistics by company, date, and type of alarm.

What type of alarm ordinance does your town have? How is the ordinance enforced? If the alarm company representative doesn't know, he or she has a problem; you should consider this when contracting for security work. For an unbiased answer, contact your local police department or state department of justice.

What type of discount will you receive for paying by cash or check? What type of discount do you receive if you pre-pay the first year of monitoring service?

Who will do the installing in your home? What are his or her credentials?

What guarantee or warranty is offered on the sensors, transfer equipment, amplifiers, and monitoring service?

Is a maintenance contract needed or included in my contract? What are the terms?

Upon installation of sensors and equipment, what responsibility will the alarm company, and the individual installer, bear should current house wiring be insufficient to support alarms and sensors? What responsibility will the company expect the homeowner to bear?

What Are You Buying?

Basically, a homeowner who leases or purchases an alarm system is paying for hardware (sensors, locks, amplifiers, etc.), installation fees, and monitoring service. An average burglar alarm system, without fire alarm application, should include:

Multi-Zone Master Control Panel. (Number of zones are dependent upon how many sensors you have installed. Each area under surveillance or "protection area," is a zone.) In a normal, two-bedroom, 2,100 square-foot home, six zones should be sufficient, absent unusually-constructed doors, garage access points, etc. It should be capable of storing up to six user codes at one time. Other requirements include battery back-up for power failure, power monitor, ability to quickly have the arm/disarm codes changed, and shunting by individual or groups of sensor zones.

One Telephone Interconnect.

One digital keypad. This is the keypad used to arm or disable your alarm system when you leave home and when you return. It should be capable of controlling all installed systems, activating duress, emergency, and duress functions, full or partial arming of perimeter sensors (shunting capability), and the complete display of system status, including power.

One 15-Watt Siren. It should be programmed with a timer, so it doesn't go on forever, once triggered. It also should have an inside speaker, to notify the owner inside the home, when activated.

Two-Four Magnetic Contacts. They should contain concealed contacts with hidden wiring.

One-Two Passive Infrared Detectors. They are for protection of interior in the event undetected entry occurs. They should detect ambient temperature changes caused by moving bodies.

One Back-up Battery and replacements.

One Transformer.

One Multi-Colored Yard Sign.

Five-Eight Window Stickers (Warning-Alarmed Residence Stickers).

Additional Equipment, *as specified in contract:*

• Audio Discriminator

• Heat/Smoke Detector

• Medical Alert Package

• Personal Duress Alarm

False Alarms

False alarms are caused by a variety of influences and events, including dense fog, the rumblings of a passing truck-and-trailer, earthquakes, and operator error. By far, operator (owner) error causes most false alarms. Either the homeowner fails to set properly the alarm when leaving the house, causing a delayed or malfunctioning alarm, or fails to disarm properly the system when entering the home, causing an immediate alarm. Besides making sure that residents know EXACTLY how to set and reset alarms, and making sure they know and remember the proper codes for setting the alarm, there are two common human errors that account for the vast majority of false alarms: carelessness and the location of the digital keypad (alarm panel).

Training, supervision, and taking time to do the job right will eliminate operator error when keying-in the subscriber code. However, placement of the digital keypad is crucial to reducing false alarms caused by operator error. Alarm panels should be located on a wall, in an area that is safe from accidental manipulation or disturbance by:

- Children. They are naturally curious, see their parents "play" with the alarm box, and by mimicking the adults, will either activate or disable the alarm.

- Pets. Dogs and cats are curious animals, especially cats, and will seek the scent of their owners on everything, including the alarm panel. By rubbing against it, they inadvertently trigger it or cause the code sequence to activate or disable the alarm.

- Water, dust and other environmental hazards. Dust caused by heavy house cleaning may disable or damage the alarm, as will the vibrations of a nearby vacuum cleaner. Excessive moisture in the air (high humidity) will affect the electronic components of a digital keypad, but only to the extent that a telephone dialing mechanism would be disturbed. Direct sunlight for prolonged periods of time, above 90 degrees F, eventually will have a disastrous effect on the digital keypad and may cause malfunction.

- Unauthorized persons. These people, out of ignorance, playfulness ("practical jokers"), maliciousness, or illegal entry into your home, may damage or disable your alarm system by keying in the wrong sequence or pushing the wrong program buttons on the digital keypad.

Alarm panels should be mounted in a place easily accessible by a person who knows the location of the panel. This location should be unobtrusive but easily reached by knowledgeable persons within fifteen (15) seconds of entering the home, so that the proper code sequence can be entered or the disable switch/button can be triggered.

It also should accomodate only those who are tall enough to reach the panel. Besides keeping children's hands from touching it, alarm panels should be placed at eye-level of the intended adult user. If this is not possible, they should be placed slightly below eye-level, since it is preferable and quicker to kneel down or slightly squat than to spend time getting something to stand on or balancing precariously while you attempt to enter a code.

Alarm panels should be mounted in an area that is well-lighted, reducing the risk of entering the wrong code sequence or hitting the wrong button/switch in the dark. They also should be positioned for easy visual identification and manipulation of the numbered keys and buttons (i.e., do not place the panel behind any object that must be moved, or moved around, to get to the panel).

· 27 ·

Voice Alarms

Not all burglar or duress alarms sound simple noises or electronic messages, such as claxons, bells, or sirens. Some receive sounds, including voice and voice commands, and transmit these sounds to a monitoring station for interpretation and comparison to pre-arranged commands.

As with all alarms, voice or voice-activated devices must be programmed to activate only upon certain conditions, such as a break in an electrical current, slipping of a magnetic connector, disruption of an infrared beam, movement of a gravity-controlled switch (stabilized mercury switch), or intentional manual activation. However, upon being triggered, voice sensors do not normally activate an alarm but transmit a series of audio impulses and begin recording sounds at the site of the sensor. It picks up human voices, including background noises, and tells the listener, usually a trained operator, what is happening. Usually, the voice alarm cannot be disconnected or stopped by anyone other than the subscriber. The monitoring operator cannot close the sensor circuit from a distant location.

An advantage of the voice alarm is that a situation can be verbally described by the subscriber, whereas a non-voice device can only transmit codified signals that must be interpreted by a monitoring operator. Another advantage is that the operator can understand, from background noises and the subscriber's verbal nuances and slang, if duress is present or if more than one person is present at the site. Also, the alarm, once triggered by the subscriber, is not normally evident or discernible at the site. The fact that the voice alarm has been triggered is not usually known to anyone else but the subscriber, thus producing a covert listening situation.

A disadvantage of the voice alarm is that some subscribers, notably the elderly, are lonely and want company and will trigger the alarm in order to talk to the monitoring operator. Another disadvantage is that the audio circuit must remain open until the subscriber closes it, thus tying up the monitoring operator's telephone line. Also, the voice sensor, if activated by mistake, can occupy the monitoring operator's telephone line for a lengthy period, until someone calls the subscriber on another telephone line or physically responds to the site and disables the sensor.

28

If the Intruder Is a
Relative or Lover

If your home intruder or attacker is a relative or has been sharing your home with you, either leave or call a friend to come stay with you. If you are a woman, you can go to a battered women's shelter, *if* there is room. The shelters are overflowing in America's cities. If you leave your home, take your children. Don't worry about getting dressed up. If it is a crisis and you are afraid, leave in your robe and slippers. For safety, it's worth it, and everyone will understand.

If you have already been a victim, go to a doctor or emergency room. Get evidence that you were beaten. Have someone take photographs of your injuries. (Don't keep the photographs at home; they could be destroyed by the attacker.) Save clothing that has been torn or blood-stained. Notify the police of the violence, and get a copy of the police report.

One problem with domestic violence is that if the perpetrator gets away with it, it most often escalates. Insist on counseling at a time when stable conversation is possible (*not* while a batterer is drunk, on drugs, or in a rage). Press charges, or press for some kind of accountability for the violent behavior. That helps bring about change. Remember, you should not be embarrassed or feel guilty that the violence becomes public. *That* is the perpetrator's fault. After physical abuse, have the abuser *move out.* Or you can move out, at least for a period of time, during counseling.

When you call the police, you should tell the dispatcher what, if any, weapons have been used, and what weapons are in the house; whether the attacker is drunk or "high"; whether you have a restraining order; or whether this has happened before. Police should take such a call far more seriously if there have been incidents before and if you give them specifics. If the police will not arrest your attacker, due to their not seeing the attack, request that a "citizen's arrest" be made. Arrest your attacker, sign a form for them, then insist they take him or her into custody and book him forthwith. Later, they may release the person if they think the charges are unfounded. Be prepared for that.

RESTRAINING ORDERS

A Temporary Restraining Order (TRO) prohibits certain behaviors of a person who has threatened you or injured you. A TRO is obtained through civil court. When you get such an order, the attacker may not come to your house, bother you at work, touch you, or call and harrass you, under penalty of being held in contempt of court. And a judge may insist that he or she moves out of your home.

This type of restraining order is for people who have been living in the same residence as the attacker. It can be enforced, even if you are not married to the attacker. You don't have to hire an attorney to get a TRO. Application forms are available in courthouses and district attorney's offices. Police also may have them, in some states. When you fill out the forms, do so very carefully. Give details. Put *copies* of other records (police reports, medical data) with the forms to bolster your case. At a hearing, the judge may order your attacker to pay out-of-pocket expenses and any wages you lost as a result of the attack.

If the attacker won't stay away from your house, call the police and tell them about the restraining order. You can go back to court and order a Contempt of Court citation. If you can't afford a lawyer, the judge may order an attorney to represent you. The attacker probably will be billed for the lawyer *and* the court costs.

If You Must Flee Your Home

If you have to leave your home because of fear of a potential attack, take the following items: your checkbook, medicine, your credit cards and driver's license, keys to your car and safe deposit box, and your address book of friends, relatives and business acquaintances. If you have a lot of time to consider fleeing, *make your Exit Box*. In it, put your insurance papers, the mortgage papers or lease to the apartment, medical records for your children, photo album, social security cards and welfare I.D., "green" card, your passport, or any other important paper you *MUST* have to function and survive over a long period of time. You can legally take anything that is yours, or yours and your husband's, or cohabiting partner's. If you share a bank account, either of you can get money out of it. If you forgot something important in your house, ask the police to escort you back inside to get it. Don't go alone. If the attacker won't allow the police to come inside, that is his or her right. There are two opposing views about whether or not police may enter the house to "keep the peace." Consult an attorney before filing charges or demanding police assistance.

Regarding your new residence: be very cautious who gets your address and phone number. (Make *certain* your children understand.) You may not want to receive mail at that address. Addresses given to the police are public record. You can use your lawyer's address on police reports or restraining orders, with his or her permission. If your car is recognizable, you may want to hide it, park it far from your new residence, or rent someone else's garage in your new neighborhood.

Finally, join a Neighborhood Watch program no matter where you are. If there is no Neighborhood Watch, *start one.* Any police agency will help. Call the Community Relations Officer or Crime Prevention Officer. After you get into the program, request—and it need not be in front of the group—that there be a special instructional program on domestic violence. Make sure that everyone attending that meeting gets a list of where to turn if he or she is a victim of domestic violence, incest, or elderly abuse. This is warning to all in your neighborhood who may be perpetrators of such crimes that the people who live on that block are prepared to act on those issues and that the local police agency knows of the neighborhood's acute interest in their enforcing domestic violence laws.

29

Legal Liability and
Home Security

Throughout HOME SAFE HOME, you have read about numerous ways to protect your home. Of concern to the courts is that frightened citizens come up with unusual ways to make themselves safe. They have been known to rig spring-guns, tripped by wires that are unseen. They have dug pits and covered them with Tarzen-like camouflage. Ground glass has been poured into freshly poured concrete on the tops of walls, spikes and slivers dangerously protruding. In civilized countries, such methods are illegal. Though they may protect against criminals, they also can injure a curious child or a foolish person—neither are criminals. So is the process by which a stranger can end up owning your house and your future income for years. When choosing security features, it is important to know the law and the liability of certain security precautions.

DANGEROUS VEGETATION

First, is there liability in using dangerous vegetation for security, cactus or bushes with long thorns? We went to the California State Bar Association for a state-wide liability expert to analyze such security features. His name is Robert Peterson, graduate of the Stanford Law School and current Dean of Santa Clara University School of Law in Santa Clara, California. Peterson is an expert on torts. (A tort is a wrongful act, for which a civil action will lie—excepted one involving breach of contract.)

Dean Peterson is not aware of any lawsuits regarding security landscaping. In regard to bushes with three-inch thorns, Peterson said, "Vegetation cannot spring up at you. It is just there. Someone must try to penetrate it." But trees that cannot hold body weight, if they look like they can (which is a pretty subjective thing), might be a risk, according to Peterson. "That is a little more like digging a pit and covering it over. Like something that disguises the fact that is dangerous. That is one of the elements that clearly constitutes 'booby-traps.' I don't know that a person would be liable for criminal prosecution for planting a brittle tree, but a homeowner would be on thinner ice, with respect to civil liability." Aside from injuring a trespasser trying to climb the tree to your second story bedroom, a branch could fall and damage a neighbor's car.

TRESPASSERS

The courts, in common law, draw distinctions between different classes of people who are on the land. In regard to security, we are talking about trespassers on the land who have no right to be there. The standard in law is, you must not willfully or wantonly injure a trespasser, but beyond that, trespassers are on your land at their own risk. Children are always an exception. In California, the state Supreme Court abolished those categories of the foolish, or children, giving a rather squishy ruling that each case must be judged on its own merits. In California, a trespasser might have more rights than he or she would have in other states because of that ruling.

CONCERTINA WIRE
FENCING

On concertina wire (coiled, circular barbed wire) for fencing, local building codes speak to its use. Concertina wire is not a trap. A fence with metal rods with points at the top is another story. A child can climb over such a fence and slip and fall, resulting in serious injury. If such a fence passes the local building code, the law leans toward the homeowner in the event of an accident.

A rule in security features is that any feature that is designed to injure an intruder could easily result in your legal liability. Security devices that make noise or dial the police, won't.

USE OF DEADLY FORCE
AGAINST AN INTRUDER

California is known for its far-sweeping legislation and court rulings. Many legal events in California tend to move across the nation, into Federal law and into the laws of other states. Regarding weapons for protection of the home and family, there is new, favorable California legislation. It is the Home Protection Bill of Rights, which was passed the same year "booby traps" were outlawed in California. The Home Protection Bill of Rights states that a California resident can use force that is intended to cause death or great bodily injury, *within* his or her residence, *if* it is presumed that he or she feared eminent peril. Another "if" regards whether the person was *not* a family member or a member of the household normally expected to be in the home. The resident using deadly force must have reason to believe that the "suspect" unlawfully or forcibly entered the home. The Home Protection Bill of Rights does not allow a loop-hole for you to finally kill ole' wife-beater, Uncle Ned, and not have to spend a few years in jail.

"While it does not give an absolute defense for use of deadly force against an intruder," Dean Peterson said, "it does create a presumption in a resident's favor, that he was in fear of death or great bodily harm. That would be justifiable homicide."

Can You Get Away with
Shooting a Burglar?

In *Gilmore vs. Superior Court*, the issue of justifiable homicide can get confusing. "In that case, a person put a ladder up to a second story window, and the homeowner noticed this person taking off a screen," Peterson said. "The homeowner ran out of his house and pulled the ladder out from under the alleged intruder. The intruder fled. As he was running away, the homeowner fired several shots. One of the bullets ricocheted and killed him. First the homeowner was prosecuted and was convicted of manslaughter. On Appeal, the defense stated that the shooting was justifiable homicide, allowing a person to attempt to arrest someone for committing a felony. The homeowner claimed to be trying to stop the alleged intruder, to arrest him."

Then there was a wrongful death suit filed against the homeowner. "Ultimately, the Court of Appeals said that if the killing were justifiable homicide on criminal actions, that there could be defense for civil action." The interesting thing about the case, according to Dean Peterson, is that the court decided that deadly force is not privileged as a matter of law in *all* cases of first degree burglary. In other words, the courts are not going to give residents *carte blanch* in their right to shoot someone attempting to burgle their homes. In the Gilmore case, they decided there was sufficient threat, but, they "waffled" a bit. The outcome was good for the homeowner, but only slightly. How could there have been sufficient threat to shoot a fleeing suspect?

"The way I read the case," Dean Peterson said, "is there was certainly no threat at the time the suspect was shot, because he was trying his best to get away; but, there was a threat at the *time* he was trying to get in. The kind of burglary for which this person could then use deadly force was termed necessary to affect an arrest. In a burglary of a car, or the burglary of an empty house, were a homeowner to come home and see the burglar in process of fleeing, the question of justifiable homicide is open. There may be no justification for shooting. The case does not give a bright line on when, and when not, to use deadly force."

The Gilmore case cites an earlier case, *Nakashima vs. Takase.* It is an old case (1935). The Gilmore court said this older case hadn't been criticized in fifty years. This case focused upon an entirely different situation. At the center was a cafe, not a residence. The owner noticed that a window had been tampered with. He suspected that the people who did it might return after hours to burglarize. "He secreted himself inside the cafe with a shotgun," Dean Peterson said. "Sure enough, some people later in the evening did break in. Once they got inside, with no warning or anything, he shot one of them. The person ultimately died. The court said that it was justifiable homicide. So, in the subsequent civil action, the court said that, as a matter of law, you couldn't recover. That seems to me like a pretty extreme situation, where the use of deadly force was justified," Peterson said.

"The court had a couple of things in the case that you might quarrel with, to get to that conclusion," Peterson added. "They said that there was force and violence used in breaking in. The defendant, as a reasonable person, had a right to assume that the two burglars were armed, even though they were not. There is an assumption that the court allowed the person to engage in, without any basis, other than the fact they broke into the cafe, that if interfered with, they would use further violence and force to consumate the theft they had planned, or to make their escape."

Based on that assumption, the court ruled for the defense. The court went on to say, aside from the fact that a death resulted, that there was no evidence that the defendant intended to kill. The attempt to protect his own property, himself, or both, does not mean he has engaged in an unlawful act. "He was simply trying to protect himself from the commission of a second felony," Peterson said. "How would the case have come out if the cafe owner had said he was attempting to kill them? Perhaps, differently."

That is the legal guidance in the State of California. It is confusing, given the law and police training. Compare yourself with a police officer in the use of deadly force. What actions you are willing to take to protect yourself and your property may become more clear.

It is generally accepted across the United States that peace officers have the right to use that force necessary to affect arrests, keep the peace, protect themselves and citizens against injury or death, and apprehend criminals. To use only the *necessary* force, and not use excessive force, requires the peace officer to be absolutely sure of what actions are happening at the time, what the law states he or she may do in that given circumstance, that they have the correct suspect (the criminal), and that the suspect has the intent and ability to resist arrest. The criminal does not need to use a weapon but may resist by merely refusing to be arrested. The peace officer must use force, in this instance, to make an arrest but may not use more force than is *minimally required*.

Keep in mind that we are talking "use of force," not "use of deadly force." The decision by a peace officer to use deadly force is anchored in the same judgemental causal factors as the decision to use force in effecting an arrest. However, two other questions must be answered when deadly force is the focal point. What alternatives could have been used (instead of deadly force), and was the officer in fear of losing his or her life? The same questions must be answered by the citizen in peril in his or her own home when confronted by an intruder.

In past legal cases involving the use of deadly force by citizens (non-police), the courts have ruled that the person in peril, in order to be justified in taking the life of another, must have had *no alternative action* available to them at the time they used the force, and they must have clearly thought that if they did not employ the force necessary to kill their attacker, they would be killed by that attacker. This focus of vulnerability is transferrable to another person, such as a loved one, a child, or a person less-capable of defending himself. This is simply stated as, "a person may kill another person to save his or her own life, or the life of another." Remember, after the smoke clears, the court must be convinced, *beyond a reasonable doubt*, that the homeowner (1) feared for his own life or the life of another, and (2) had no alternative force available. If these two factors are proven in court, the homicide will, most likely, be declared justifiable, or done in self-defense. There are no other decisions, other than guilty of murder, manslaughter, or by medical mis-adventure.

If you are sued over your actions after using force on an intruder, it pays to know what lawsuits are like. For those who have been through them, it is like spending years with periodic trips to hell, paying for the transportation there, and having everyone else connected to hell having power over you, your bank account, your schedule, your relationship with loved ones, how well you do at work under the stress, and your future. Having to act quickly when an intruder comes into your bedroom at 4:00 AM, it may be hard to sort out all you must consider. Police have to make decisions that may make them vulnerable to lawsuit many times each day. They have received hundreds of hours of training on such decisions and what to avoid; and then repeatedly, they are told to avoid the most dangerous acts. And, they *still* get sued. It pays to think a little on this issue *before* an emergency arises.

30

Security for the Aged
and the Disabled

A crook doesn't look for another crook as victim. He looks for someone less street-wise than himself. He seeks someone weak and easy to dominate. Women make better victims than men. Older women are easier victims than younger women. And elderly men are better targets than healthy young men. Yet, it is teenaged males who are most likely to become crime victims because of their heightened activity, in general, and because theirs is a more violent generation. Their victimization is not necessarily linked to their role as weaker "prey." Elderly citizens are more likely to be victims when a gun is used during the commission of a crime.

Statistics say the number of traditional nuclear families of mother, father and children living under one roof is dwindling. This has had an impact on crime against older Americans. Years ago, older relatives were taken into the homes of their grown children, or they lived a few blocks away. Today, children leave the nest and travel thousands of miles away from home, or, the older parent leaves the support group in the hometown and moves to a warmer climate where virtually no one checks on them, other than by telephone. Older roommates, such as "The Golden Girls" on television, each protecting one another, sharing experiences and having mutual concern about the well-being of one another, is not yet the norm. For safety, there must be a substitute for a family's watching over an older relative. Read on:

1. Many older people are victims when someone follows them home or sees them on the street. To reduce that threat, many older people refrain from leaving their residence unescorted. There remains a feeling that there is safety in numbers. That is not always true, but having another person with you is better than being alone. Here is how the crook looks at it. A single victim is preferable to two or more victims together, because more victims also can mean more resistance. Certainly, the crook would rather face one person in court than several who can identify him. An elderly person in the city out after dark might as well be wearing a revolving red light and carrying a speaker shouting, "Easy pickings. Come and get it." Venturing out at night may mean you will be followed back home. It is best not to do it.

If you must go out after dark, walk with purpose, like someone who can take care of himself. (If you have a walker or cane, *please* ask someone else to go to the store for you at night.) For the elderly, who often are less sure-footed, after injury or illness, there is a tendency to look down at the sidewalk while walking to avoid hazards. Even a small crack or rise in the sidewalk can mean a broken hip for an older person. However, in spite of that concern there should be effort not to keep the head down all the time. Scan the environment around you. If someone passes you, make limited eye contact, but don't stare. The purpose of this is to let someone know you see them, that you can recognize them later (in court), and that you are in possession of your faculties.

Avoid smiling at everyone you meet, no matter how sunny your disposition. In today's world, a friendly person can be taken for a "sap," just another trusting soul who makes a great victim.

Avoid greeting everyone you meet. Instead of saying to a stranger, "Hello. Isn't it a beautiful morning?" simply say, "Morning." You will appear to be more street-wise and in tune with today and the dangers on the street. Keep going as you pass people. Do not stop and engage in conversation with strangers no matter how wonderful or how lonely you feel. Act as if you don't have time to chit-chat, that someone may be waiting for you. You can even wave to an imaginary friend or glance at a watch, as if you are waiting for someone.

2. Carry something in your hand that can be used as a weapon. No, you don't have to lug a mini-tank, rocket-launcher, or bow and arrows, although there are many things that can fend off an attacker. A hefty swing with a clipboard can get someone's attention very quickly. A hard-bound book can be an effective weapon, if used confidently. At night, a flashlight is justified and becomes a dependable weapon. Practice with it. So can a large, ballpoint pen or a full softdrink can. A simple pack of playing cards can be used to rake across a person's face, to "load" a punch to the stomach or the groin. Remember, you must be legally justified to defend yourself. You must be fending off a physical attack.

Chicago police sergeant Richard Doyle said he knew a nurse who carried a brick to and from trips out of her home. He laughed when he told the story, but he was intrigued with the nurse's strategy. "She said, 'Everytime I leave home, I carry the brick, and I carry it right in my hand. If anybody tries to assault me, I'll throw it through the first window I find. If it's a house, I'm going to draw somebody's attention, and if it's a business, an alarm will go off.' When you think about it," Doyle said, "it's common sense. Realizing that there are people out there who want what you have. You have to be a little bit smarter than they are."

3. Wear good walking shoes, nothing flimsy that you can't run in, or get you footing in an emergency. Heavy shoes will cause damage to a mugger's groin, while slippers or sandals will only make him angry. Another good idea is to wear a second layer of clothing over your torso, a light jacket if it is a hot day, heavier if the weather is cool. (Use discretion. You don't want to get heat stroke.) This gives an extra layer of protection between your skin and a fist or weapon of an attacker. Criminals use this trick all the time. With an older person, grabbing an arm roughly, given an extra "buffer" of clothing, may prevent a bone fracture. Wearing a hat, taking it off and swinging it in multiple strokes will distract an attacker and also will draw attention from passersby.

4. When you must leave your house, don't advertise to casual acquaintances where you are going or when you will be back. Don't make it easy for a crook to lay in wait. Keep your business to yourself and your trusted friends. *Do* let one of those trusted friends know when you are coming and going. Advise them to call the police if you are not home by a certain hour. Call this person if you will be late.

5. Don't wear expensive jewelry or clothing or allow your purse or wallet to show. Turn your rings around, in public. If you carry a purse, keep the strap snug around your shoulders, across the chest, with the purse in front, not at the side. Keep a wallet in a front pants pocket, not in the rear where it can be slipped out by a thief. Never count money in front of strangers. You can try a trick the women in the inner-city have been using for years. Make a little pocket on the inside of your bra. Carry folding money there. It's best *not* to get it out at the check-out stand in the supermarket. That little pocket is a secret. (*Caution: if someone fights for your purse, surrender it quickly.* It is no longer unusual for a woman to be killed for her purse.)

6. If you are out at night, stay in lighted areas.

7. If you use bus transportation, don't use stops that are dimly lighted. Use bus stops where a lot of people congregate or pass. Don't get your money out in front of strangers. Have it ready, in a pocket. Sit as close to the busdriver as you can get. If you are afraid of someone, wait until the bus stops and change seats. If someone bumps into you, check to see if you still have your wallet or purchased items.

Pickpockets work buses daily. While you are out, don't strain to see streetsigns or look lost. A crook will know you are new in the area, don't know where you are going, and that you are vulnerable.

For organized solutions to crimes against the elderly, there are some wonderful programs out there. Among the most exciting solutions, it is the elderly themselves who are providing the protection.

THE RSVP AND
YANA PROGRAMS

In San Clemente, California, the police department has the RSVP, or Retired Senior Volunteer Program. It's a crime prevention unit that sets an outstanding example for community policing: attacking crime with trained volunteers and a lot of attention to those most likely to be "prey."

RSVP volunteers are uniformed, and they go out in pairs,

like police officers. They drive a marked patrol car. They do not carry guns but are professionally trained to report crimes. Each volunteer is asked to donate six hours a week. The participants conduct security surveys, present Neighborhood Watch programs, make vacation checks on homes, and visit or phone elderly residents who are homebound. Many seniors are involved as volunteers. Better yet, the RSVP group has the "You Are Not Alone" program. Called YANA, every morning, elderly citizens are greeted with a "good morning" call from YANA volunteers. Expanded service includes visits to the homes of bedridden citizens or those merely living alone. Gradually, a strong network of citizens caring for other citizens has emerged. Friendships have formed, or for want of a better word, a "family." The police department supervision flows from a police lieutenant and a sergeant. There is a monthly meeting between volunteers and police professionals about needs in the community, training, etc. San Clemente has 24 RSVP volunteers, and they have given 6,000 hours of service in one year. It's a boon for the elderly and a big savings to taxpayers. It also is rewarding work for older American's who want to stay involved in very challenging, rewarding activity.

In Reedley, California, a similar program sprang up, with volunteers receiving 25 hours of training. They also work in pairs. Their cars are unmarked. These volunteers work four-hour shifts, patrolling on foot during the holiday season, a high-crime period. Reedley's volunteers have put in over 4,000 hours of service, done 1,697 vacation house checks, accumulated 476 visits to elderly citizens and performed 93 courier trips. This is an extended "family" for older Americans. It makes their lives safer.

Cities or retirement communities wanting more information about starting RSVP service groups may contact the Community Relations Officers of the San Clemente and Reedley, California, Police Departments.

Advice for Older Americans
From Security Experts

From John H. Conley, Certified Protection Professional of Des Moines, Iowa. "Elderly people are "muscled" easily, so they have to be careful who they allow in their homes. A big problem is that many older Americans are very lonely. They want conversation. Someone, *anyone* to talk to, can be a pleasant sight. They need to be cautious and ask, 'Who are you? What do you want?' If someone comes to the door and says they are selling insurance, tell them you'll talk to them about it on the telephone. *Don't let anyone you don't know come into your home.* Make sure you have a peephole so you don't have to open the door to a stranger. Once the door is open, they can push their way inside. If someone claims to have an emergency and needs to use the telephone, *don't* open the door. Ask for the telephone number. Make the call yourself, or call the police for help. And phone a nearby relative or friend that someone is there."

Jerry L. Wright, Certified Protection Professional, of Ann Arbor, Michigan

"Personal safety is a state of mind. You do that which makes you feel comfortable in your environment. What are the special problems of older people? Quite often, the senior person is intimidated by what they have seen on television. It can lead to isolation. A new concern, due to the collapse of the savings and loan industry, more seniors are now keeping their money at home, rather than depositing it. It's similar to what happened in America during the Thirties. It makes people targets of crime. Due to a fixed income, seniors can be vulnerable to making a quick buck in a short amount of time, to augment that fixed income. I've known intelligent seniors with common sense, who have fallen victim because a scam was so unique in terms of marketing. They fell for it. Those are my cautions.

In terms of diminishing sight, hearing and strength, an older person has to think about how to take control of their environment. I was in a shopping mall one time, and I witnessed a young man approach an elderly women. He was about eight feet away, when she turned and yelled, 'GET THE HELL OUTTA' HERE,' at the top of her lungs. The young man immediately moved away. He had gotten into her zone of comfortability. Basically, she wasn't going to allow herself to be victimized. In sexual assault cases, I have instructed women to stand in front of the mirror and make eye-to-eye contact and learn how to yell, 'NO.' Give commands. Showing authority rather than intimidation, where your eyes drop or you look at the ground, showing you are vulnerable. You have to look like you are in control. Afterwards, you can do what everyone does, 'crash' with your legs shaking, and think of what *could* have happened. But, for that moment, you were guided by survival."

SECURITY HARDWARE

It is not enough to consult security experts and police on personal security needs of the aged or disabled. If you, or someone you care about is in either, or both, of these categories, you will have special concerns. Some security features and hardware can be a danger for some people.

To better understand these concerns, we consulted both handicapped individuals and a top occupational therapy supervisor from Cedar Sinai Medical Center. Camille Tareshawty, who is an expert on the disabled, has worked not only with the financially privileged which Cedar Sinai serves, but she has also worked in rural Kentucky. Ms. Tareshawty explains what she and her subordinates do to make sure a home is safe for an injured or aged person. While reading the following, it is important to consider buttons on alarm panels that need to be pushed, special locks that need unlocking, window latches for security, etc., and what problems they present to a person who has special needs.

"We take patients into their homes and watch them perform tasks in that environment," Tareshawty said. "We also do that without the patient. We look at the width of doorways for use of a walker or wheelchair. We make sure furniture is arranged so a person has access easily, without continually being put into a position of risk. On a routine basis, no arrangement should set them up for an accident if they need to move quickly, or if they are fatigued. We see where things are plugged in. We look to see how far a favorite chair is from the bathroom. We look at safety steps and rails coming into the home or apartment. Throw rugs for decoration may cause them to trip or catch a walker. We look at thresholds. We've seen some up to an inch high. Cabinets have to be arranged into work stations. All supplies for baking go together, so they don't have to cross a kitchen to get a pan, then walk back across to get the mixer. If the person has a decreased reach or a decreased range of motion in the shoulders, we have to assess if they can safely lower a heavy object. How are things arranged so that they can smoothly conduct their lives?

"If you do not have access to an occupational therapist, first analyze the home of the aged or disabled person, or your own home, if you or a relative has special needs. The home, first, has to be safe, before security issues are addressed.

"I would like you to think about being on cruthes, in a wheelchair, or using a cane. Think of the organization of this situation: having a bag of groceries, opening a screendoor, finding your keys, putting your keys in the lock, *while* keeping the screendoor open, pushing the door open without losing your balance forward, and getting yourself through that doorway. *Anything* you do to add security to that door, decreases your ease at entering. It compounds the amount of organization, strength and balance you must have, to get inside."

Many times, a person who has a disability is intelectually intact. There are disabilities with strokes or brain injuries that may *not* be readily evident. A security expert must realize, or you must realize, if you are handling the security needs, that you do not compromise safety by adding complications a person with injury may not figure out, once alone.

If a person is on medication, that further complicates security. Everyday routines like picking up a washcloth and washing the face may be difficult to perform. Motor planning, sequencing, what to do if water is hot, can be a problem. That is learned at three or four years-old, but a person with cognitive disability may find that simple task difficult, and they also may find it hard to push a specific button to unlock a door. During an emergency, that button could compromise their ability to open the door to get out.

Tareshawty says that in health care right now, many of the decisions about when a person leaves a hospital, is driven by reimbursement. Patients are now sent home when they can be safely cared for. Previously, patients were sent home when they could function alone. Due to the economic crunch, a lot of disabled or injured people are not home alone. In regard to security, that is good.

As far as security equipment is concerned, a cellular telephone is one of the most important security features for anyone and especially for an aged or disabled person. They can be hooked to a wheelchair, or even a walker, with special equipment that resembles a sock with a hook. The wireless phone goes into it. "But, most of our elderly population is not enthralled with gadgets," Tareshawty said. "I think, in the next decade, we will see more openness to that. They will have grown up with those things. Now we have 80- and 90-year-olds who don't have cordless phones, and they don't want them." (A caution: cordless phones can be dangerous with their long antennas. As a patient becomes more mobile, the antennae gets caught on things.)

It is very important that an aged or disabled person be tested on the operations of locks, *any* lock or latches they must use. Injury does not only decrease strength, it also affects coordination, depth perception and a person's ability to understand sequence. After a stroke or a brain injury, there can be problems with problem solving. "If you were confronted with a situation, and you approached it in a routine way . . . and the way you approached that problem didn't work for you, *you* would generate other alternatives. You would choose the best option, try it, go to yet another option," Tareshawty said. "Sometimes, with neurological deficits, a person loses that ability to solve certain problems. Locks, smoke alarms, gates that lock in a complicated way, can be a very serious problem for persons with neurological deficits." Tareshawty suggests that each situation be presented so that the disabled person be allowed to learn to work through the problem rather than having to do so during an emergency. Security experts told us that it would be important to present such problems often enough that a change in physical or mental condition would be noticed.

With security shutters, many disabled people have trouble opening a stuck window. Opening or closing a security shutter could be worse because it would require a lot of standing balance. The frail elderly person has neither balance nor strength. "If we set things up to give the body the best advantage," Tareshawty instructs, "we don't end up doing our heavy work at the end of a reach, instead of mid-line where we are stronger. At the end of a reach, there is decreased strength." Consider this when installing any security feature to the home of an aged or disabled person. A person may be able to lift that much weight during a test, but if it is not in "mid-line" and their body isn't in an advantageous place, they lose all the ability to do that lift. The most advantageous position to increase arm strength? With the elbow supported on a table or counter, with the person standing. The arm then works like a lever.

31

Security for the
Sightless

Among those we interviewed to better understand security problems of the vision-impaired was Sue Earhart, a young blind woman who was the victim of attempted rape. In this case, the rapist was a former employee of a business that provides services to the blind. The assailant made no noise when he came into her bedroom at night. Ms. Earhart's said that her only clue that someone might be in the room was that when she arose to walk to the hallway, her guide dog hesitated, stopped every few steps. She could not get him to move. Yet he didn't bark, nor did he try to protect her in any way.

She was finally grabbed and forced down. She says that she was so terrified that she treated her assailant like "the Emperor Royal," then distracted him. The police responded and saved her, she says, when someone close by heard her initial scream. "I didn't panic."

The visually impaired have special problems with security. One of the most valuable security items for a visually impaired person is a cellular phone. Another is a duress alarm. Neither is cheap. A blind person, one with a white cane or a Seeing Eye Dog, is easily targeted by a criminal. There is a tentative movement and slow travel that is inviting to someone looking for prey. What, then, can be done to enhance security?

1. Police whistles make a shrill, loud noise. The black plastic ones cost around two dollars, and those made of brass usually cost less than five dollars. It is easy to make a necklace out of a police whistle. Use a ribbon or a gold chain, or glue rhinestones on it. If you don't think it looks chic, take it off at parties or weddings, but keep it in your pocket. When things are less formal, put it back on. But do not go outside without it. Make your neighbors aware that a good blow on that police whistle means you are in trouble. 'Come quick or call the police.' More expensive is a "screamer," which emits a deafening sound. It activates when you press a button. You can carry a "screamer" with you as you walk down the street or take out the garbage. Again, make sure your neighbors know what the sound is in case you need to alert them to an attack or a home intrusion.

2. Be knowledgeable about assault. Knowledge is power. Most sexual assaults occur in a victim's home, in a garage or a laundry room of an apartment building. Those are the most dangerous places. Rape is the fastest growing crime in the United States, and more startling is that over 50 percent of the rapes committed are committed by someone who knows the victim. Rapists look like everyone else. They may be married or have been very active in religious activities; a rapist could be the rug cleaner next door. Rape is *not* motivated by sexual desire. It is a violent act, whereby an assailant seeks to humiliate or hurt his victim. It doesn't matter how unattractive a victim may be, how old, or that they have body odor that could knock over a horse. A rapist has a sick desire to injure. *Anyone* can be a victim of a rapist. There was once a rapist who chose only women who wore white dresses. You could be the next woman in a white dress who walked past his car. Be aware.

3. If you live in multi-unit housing, let another person know when you are going to the laundry room. These days it is a good idea to ask someone to accompany you to the laundry room. When you leave a communal laundry room, leave a light on. Yes, it wastes electricity, but light is a deterrant to crime. If other residents leave the door unlocked to the laundry room, make a point of demanding it stop. Draw on their understanding, that you have special problems with personal security, that you need help. Tell them HOME SAFE HOME made the recommendations.

4. When you are outside, walk close to the curb, not close to buildings, doorways and alleys. If someone stops, do not go close to the car. It is too easy to be dragged inside. Stay your distance.

5. If you think you are in danger, don't be shy or embarrassed. Scream. Yell "Fire." And don't stop screaming until you get a lot of attention or until the police come.

6. Don't go places alone. Invest in friendships with people who have the freedom in their lifestyles to go places with you. This is the best deterrent of all.

7. If someone calls your home or comes to your door, *never* let them know you are alone. "My husband is home with the flu. I'm busy." *"We're* expecting company very soon. I'm sorry, I can't talk." If necessary, talk to your "invisible friend." "Honey, there's someone at the door for you. My husband can't come to the door, right now. He's giving our dog a bath."

8. Always have your keys ready when you enter your home. Don't leave yourself in a position where you have to search for them after you arrive. (If you are attacked, keys can be a weapon, pointed ends out, scrape the face and aim for the eyes.) Have the entry door area well-lit *at all times*, even at night after you are in bed.

9. If you come home and you can tell someone has entered your home, DO NOT GO INSIDE. Go to a neighbor or a phone booth nearby and call the police. Have the police check inside before you re-enter.

10. Instruct your children, relatives or home employees *never* to give out information over the telephone. (Where you are, when you will be back, where you are going, whether "the man of the house is in.")

In recent months, there have been crimes where assailants posed as police officers, complete with uniforms and badges. If someone comes to your door or approaches you and they claim to be police, realize that anyone can buy a badge and a uniform. They can be purchased at uniform shops or even stolen. There is great concern on the West Coast because in several instances during 1992 hundreds of police uniforms have been stolen in burglaries of cleaning establishments. In those burglaries, it was the *uniforms* that were the main targets. Badges, gunbelts, etc. have been stolen from uniform shops in several cities. Add to that enormous amounts of ammunition and firearms that have been stolen in burglaries. Where are those uniforms to be used? Will they be sold "underground" across the nation? No one knows, but something is in the works. Before you trust that a person is a police officer, call the local police department and ask if they have an Officer "So and So." Inform the Desk Officer or the Watch Commander that the officer is at your door. In addition, do not trust that because a person wears a utility company uniform that he is what he says he is. Check before you cooperate. Get the telephone numbers from the operator if you must. Do not take the number from that person. He could have an accomplice at the other end of the phone line.

If you have a seeing eye dog, realize that the dog, though usually good-sized, was not selected for aggressive qualities. Dogs with "fight" wash out of seeing eye dog school. During the commission of a crime, he may remain docile. He was chosen for that quality, and he has been trained to remain that way. Then again, he is still a dog and may tear the face off an intruder. If he does not, understand why. He's not a regular dog. He's very special.

· 32 ·

Security Expert on

the Hearing Impaired

Officer Dan Levin, Preventive Programs/Chicago Police Academy

For years, the Chicago Police Department had a special unit assigned to handle crimes against the disabled. The officers selected for such duty were chosen for having special sensitivity toward that segment of the population. Among those officers was Dan Levin. The birth of his specialty began one day when Levin handled a police call involving a deaf woman. She was a victim of on-going vandalism. Levin knew finger spelling but didn't know sign language. Since the crime required a number of visits to the home to catch the suspect, Levin started learning sign language. "After a few months," he told us, "I learned enough signs to ask her out." And, after several years of dating, they were married. And so began the career of Dan Levin, who is now a police academy instructor on helping deaf people who are victims, or witnesses, of crimes. Since his wife is "profoundly deaf, and her two sisters are deaf, her mother was deaf, and her father, she also has deaf aunts, uncles and cousins," Levin now has a unique position in learning about victimization of the "hearing impaired." He also has much to share with both police officers across the nation and with people who cannot hear or who cannot hear *well* enough to be safe.

"First of all, deaf people are at risk. They tend to be out and about, just like the rest of the population," Levin said.

"Most sexual assaults of the deaf that I have handled, have involved deaf suspects, persons known to the deaf person." Other than being very selective about companions, there are specific things a hearing-impaired person can do to enhance security. "A Hearing Ear Dog is a good first step in living defensively. "Interestingly, one of the most used features of a Hearing Ear Dog, is letting the deaf person know when they've dropped their keys. A deaf person can't hear them hitting the ground."

Not everyone is yet aware of the existence of Hearing Ear Dogs. Sometimes it is necessary for a hearing-impaired person to educate mall owners and restaurant managers of their use, for the animal to be welcomed. The dogs are trained with sound work, such as door knocks, the telephone, and fire or burglar alarms. Dogs for the Deaf choose animals from shelters. After a medical examination and evaluation of temperment, they go into puppy raising homes. There the puppies are taught simple obedience, manners and socialization. At eight to twelve months old, they go into advanced training.

Executive Director Robin Dickson of Dogs for the Deaf in Central Point, Oregon, said that Hearing Ear Dogs have the same legal access rights as Seeing Eye Dogs. They can go anyplace a deaf person goes. Unfortunately, each state has its own law regarding Hearing Ear Dogs. Dickson has lobbied to bring about uniformity in those laws and continues to fight for Federal legislation to bring about a national standard for dogs that aid the hearing-impaired. Each state has minor differences in their laws, which causes deaf people problems. Hawaii was the last state to give access rights, during the summer of 1992.

Most dogs at the Oregon Training Center are under thirty pounds. This is not a big business, and there will be a waiting list at most Hearing Ear Dogs associations. The Oregon operation, founded by Robin Dickson's father, screens potential recipients to make certain there is truly a hearing impairment and that a Hearing Ear Dog is actually necessary for normal living. Dogs for the Deaf places only forty-five dogs a year. A hearing impaired person who wants a Hearing Ear Dog must submit to personal interviews, one of which is in the home. There is careful screening to make sure the commitment to the animal is loving and well thought out. Then, when a good match between dog and human is made, a trainer goes to the hearing impaired person's home and works with the new team for a week. There is on-going follow-up and evaluation through the life of the animal, which includes proof of proper medical care. Only a person who can financially afford to take care of a Hearing Ear Dog properly can get an animal. The Hearing Ear Dog brings love, sound awareness, freedom and greatly enhanced security. And in the process, many loving animals are rescued from animal shelters.

A caution: Hearing Ear Dogs are not protection dogs. They are not trained for that. Their value is that they function as the human's ears. They have the same deterrent value as a family pet. Many a burglar, when he hears a dog barking inside, will move on to burgle the next house. The dog will alert the human that someone is breaking in. They are trained to notify of noise or events.

If someone is sneaking up behind you, you may be able to hear him. A deaf person has no such advantage. The dog allows a deaf person to know what is going on around him or her. There is security going to sleep at night because the dog notifies of an alarm.

To find out more about Hearing Ear Dogs, contact the nonprofit association, Dogs for the Deaf in Central Point, Oregon. Ms. Dickson says there is no charge to a deaf person, other than maintenance, for a Hearing Ear Dog. All funding is provided by donations.

The Hearing Impaired and Police

Officer Levin advises hearing-impaired persons to contact their local police departments, especially if they live in small cities. "Make sure they know how to use TTD equipment, which allows a deaf person to type over telephone lines. Oftentimes, a department may have the equipment, but personnel may not be sufficiently trained. They may not know how to recognize a TTD call." Levin mentioned a case in one larger city, where a deaf person called several times, and the police agency personnel hung up on him. The result? By the time he called for help elsewhere, and *that* person called the police, it was too late. Someone died. Levin said that deaf residents should check with their police agency to make sure the equipment is maintained. "Deaf advocacy groups can help them do that," he said.

The Law and Sign Language
Interpreters for Police

Hearing impaired persons should check with their city government to ensure that sign language interpreters are available to local police, as required by law. "Section 504 of the Federal Rehabilitation Act, and now the new one, the Americans with Disabilities Act, requires it," Levin said. "Police departments are required to have a sign language interpretor, they must have a written policy on it, and the police officers must know the services available. The interpreter must be *qualified*, not just a person who knows sign language," Levin emphasized. The police agency is required by law to pay the interpreters. "It is very important," Levin said, "that when a deaf person is a victim of a crime, or is a witness to a crime, that the police don't arrive and say, 'Now what?'"

Why is the sign language interpreter so important? An inappropriate person who serves as interpreter can clog up the wheels of justice and render a good case useless. "Family members should *not* be used as interpreters," Levin said. "You may be dealing with bias. Ninety-five percent of the families of deaf people don't even know sign language. If they do, they may not know it well enough to interpret accurately." Levin illustrates potential problems with a story about a young deaf girl.

"She was a deaf incest victim whose mother was interpreting for her in court. The mother was saying the girl was sorry, that she was lying, and that she'd made the whole thing up. The judge held the case over. During the weekend, he got another interpreter. He found out the following Monday, that the girl was beaten by the mother over the weekend. In this case, the mother didn't want to lose her 'meal ticket.' That's not the only problem. You never want to use a child of a deaf person to interpret either. Especially in a domestic situation. 'Mommy caught Daddy with Mommy's best friend.' You don't want a ten-year-old child to interpret on that. A ten-year-old child won't have the vocabulary or the legal concepts to explain the word 'summons,' or the legal remedies available.

"Often, a police officer will think he can write to communicate with a deaf person. Unfortunately, deaf people are often pre-lingually deaf. They generally learn English as a second language. Their first language is American sign language. That has a different structure than English. It is more closely related to French than it is to English."

Levin says that many deaf people will not be able to communicate *effectively* in written English. "You can't Mirandize a deaf person by showing them the Miranda warnings on a pre-printed card. The warnings must be interpreted for the deaf person. I ask recruits, 'How would you like to go through a police investigation in your high school Spanish?'"

Another bit of advice for police: Levin says, "It is important that police departments know where these people live. They need to be aware of the legal and operational requirements of dealing with deaf people."

Alarms and Other Security Products for the Hearing Impaired

There are now many alarms for aid to the deaf: flashing light alarms, baby-cry signaling devices, smoke alarms with flashing lights and strobe lights. Signaling devices are around thirty dollars. Most are wireless. It will not be difficult for a deaf person to find products of special use to them. Many are sold through the mail. One such vendor is the House of the Deaf in Chicago. Contact your local library, ask for the reference librarian, and seek help in finding the local or state advocacy group for the hearing-impaired. They will help you.

Keeping Private

Conversations Private

The following electronic devices protect privacy:

VOCO MASK 1000 has sixteen different voice levels. Under the flip cover, switches can be moved to make your voice sound like a man, woman or child. The unit inserts between a telephone handset and base. This style of hook-up increases the quality of the voice change over the simple coupler device used by other units.

The *DIGITAL VOICE CHANGER* allows you either to place or receive telephone calls without being recognized. If you are an elderly woman, or a woman afraid of being taken advantage of, this device is of immeasurable value. Feminine voices can be made to sound masculine. Battery powered, it can fit in your pocket and has a velcro strap that attaches to any phone. Push the DOG button, and a dog barks. It sells for under four hundred dollars.

The *AUDIO JAMMER* keeps conversations private. It generates a random sound that desensitizes near-by microphones. It also protects against microwave or laser-reflection telephone pickups. The sound from the jammer varies randomly in frequency and amplitude. It has a control that allows you to set the level of protection. One unit will protect up to 150 sq. ft. Illustrations come with the unit to suggest placement of the units. Powered by a 9-volt alkaline battery, which is included. Weighs 7 ounces. It sells for less than three hundred dollars.

TELEPHONE PRIVACY MODULE helps prevent eavesdropping by family members, guests or employees. With a

TPM⁻ on each telephone in the house, the first person to pick up the receiver is the only one who can have use of the line. No one can listen on other extensions. It installs with a modular jack on one end and a modular plug on the other end for single-line (non-party line) telephones and costs less than twenty dollars.

TAP TRAP WIRETAP DETECTOR checks phone lines for on-premises series and parallel bugs and wiretaps. It also checks for hookswitch bypasses, which is a modification to the telephone so that a transmitter or dynamic earphone can pick up room sounds, then pass them down the phone line to a listening post, even when the phone is hung up. Detects series devices with resistance of 61 OHMS or more. Most have resistance of 100 OHMS. It also detects parallel devices with resistance of 65 MEGOHMS, or less. (Most parallel taps are under 30 MEGOHMS.) Weighing seven ounces, it comes with plugs, cords, adapters, battery and manual and sells for less than two hundred dollars.

TRANSTEC RF BUG DETECTOR combines a radio frequency transmitter detector, a transmitter monitor and a radio frequency sweep-device into one unit. Uses non-alarming signals, a blinking LED read-out, and a vibrating device. The TRANSTEC can be worn, signaling presence of a transmission, without revealing its use. It allows extraneous transmissions to be heard over an earphone and is particularly useful if an advance electronic sweep is impossible.

When you lift the telephone receiver, the *PHONE GUARD* checks the line for simple taps or off-the-hook telephones. If either is detected, the privacy light goes out and the phone is muted. Dial a switch, and the Phone Guard scans the radio spectrum for operating wireless microphones hidden inside the telephone or nearby. After you place a call, you switch the Phone Guard to its next duty, which uses a DC clamp restricting available power on the line, turning off taps and recorders. "Mode Three" also activates a noise generator (background baffle). Powered by a 9-volt battery (not included). Portable. Costs less than four hundred dollars.

DESVideo surveillance is legal in most states. the *VCD-4^* helps you find out if you are the subject of hidden surveillance cameras. Video cameras radiate a signal, which the VCD-4^ picks up and converts to an audible tone, which is heard in earphones (included). The tone gets louder as you approach the camera site. With a detection range of 20 feet, it only weighs seven ounces. It comes with battery, earphones and manual and sells for less than three hundred dollars.

These products are available at selected finer jewelry stores nationwide and The Spy Factory, headquartered in San Antonio, Texas. Stated prices are subject to change by the retailer.

· 34 ·

How to Protect Yourself Against the Worst of Enemies

Today's headlines scream of home invasions, random shootings of strangers, kidnappings, child-molesting rings, rapes and murders committed by the uncaring and unrepentent—people who commit violent acts for recreation, revenge, greed or merely convenience. That cold-hearted group is growing because of the breakdown of the family, violence, drugs, dwindling education and job resources. A heightened feeling of fear and isolation has been spreading across the United States stemming from increased numbers of crimes, the viciousness with which those crimes are committed, and the seeming inability of anyone, from police to politicians, to stop it. According to a study by the National Victim Center in Washington DC, fear of crime already has dramatically altered the way Americans live their lives. Nearly 80 percent of the women questioned claim to limit where they go by themselves because they are afraid. Nearly 40 percent of the men claimed to do so, as well. Sadly, the projections by police are that crime is going to grow worse as we approach the year 2000. If you can no longer feel safe walking down your own street, shopping at the corner market, or sitting on your front porch on a hot summer evening, how will you cope with those changes in lifestyle? Must you be responsible for your own protection? To a great degree, yes. Police are under-resourced, and as crime rates rise, business interests leave the area for safer environments. The city's tax bases shrink, making them cut law enforcement budgets even further. As police budgets are slashed, fewer officers cover more territory, allowing the crime rate to continue to rise, resulting in increases in calls for police service. It becomes a vicious cycle, and you are the victim. Aside from the crime rate, many people have had enemies, sometimes enemies they don't even know. Employees go gunning for bosses, citizens strike back at the state by taking a shot at a civic official, a former husband goes after the wife's new boyfriend. Police in cities are fired upon, followed home, and ambushed. As societies' structures break down and people grow more frustrated, acts of violence tend to increase. If you are a person who is someone's target, what do you do? Where do you start?

Divide your life-style into protection zones, such as home, travel, leisure, work, wandering, etc. Although changes in behavior can have the strongest affect on personal safety, those persons who can afford security hardware have many more options. Each protection zone in your daily life has different security requirements, some of which overlap but may employ different tools or products to accomplish the same thing. For example, access security at home and at work may be similar, but one may require a built-in alarm system where the other may only need a portable alarm system. Also, intruder detection at home may be somewhat different than intruder detection at work but may be very similar while traveling or while staying in a hotel. Each protection zone has a definite objective (KEEPING YOU SAFE), while the methods and mechanics may differ.

If you are someone's target, you can learn a lot from police. Law enforcement officers must worry about unsavory characters who might trail them home and kill their spouse, threaten the children, or smash the car windows with a baseball bat. There are occasions when big city police officers or private investigators must live differently than you do. It is the nature of the work—survival in the jungle. Here is the way they survive if there is bad guy out to get them, or one rich enough from drug profits to *pay* someone to get them. If you are a controversial public official in need of privacy, a film star whose home is repeatedly broken into by an obsessive fan, the victim of a stalker, or a tired parent fleeing from a drug-crazed adult child, read carefully. You *can* make your own life easier.

First, you must administratively isolate yourself from the person or persons who might try to attack you or your residence. The trick is not to let them discover where you live. Finding out where you live is simple; a person simply checks the telephone book, post office, utility companies, and other places that regularly list names and addresses. It is amazing what information clerks and receptionists will divulge when coaxed or "gag called" by a professional. *Virtually any and all information can be obtained.* You have to eliminate the possibility that a clerk or receptionist *has* the information to give. They can't give out what they don't have.

Do not list your utilities or your telephone in your name. Have a close friend register for electrical, gas, telephone, and water service at your address. It must be a close friend, because he or she is depending upon you not to ruin their credit, and also, this close friend must trust that what you are doing is important, if unorthodox.

Do not receive your mail at your residence. Contract with a private mailbox company (they are everywhere) to receive all your mail. The best services offer around-the-clock mail service; i.e., you are provided a key to the outer door and a key to your own mailbox, and you can gather your mail at your convenience, not just when the mailbox company is open for business. When applying for this private mailbox service, *list your business address and telephone number on the application form, not your residence.* Remember, you are trying to protect your residence, not your work address. If someone should happen to gain access to this application form, it will not reveal your home address but will send them back to your business site. Do not list your home telephone number ON ANYTHING.

Conceal your home address from those folks at the Department of Motor Vehicles. The DMV is an excellent source of information for private investigators, since most DMV employees are paid low wages and some are always on the lookout for a way to earn extra money. The relaying of your name, address and motor vehicle description takes only a few seconds and can bring in one-hundred dollars from a private investigator. No one is the wiser, and it can't be proven where the information was obtained. Don't give the DMV clerk the information to set you up. Since it is a crime in nearly all states to obtain a driver license under a false name, list only your mailbox address when applying for or renewing your license. The idea is to protect your residence.

Protecting your car, and its connection to you, is another matter. If you are really serious about severing ties with anything on public record, there is a way to do this. You must decide, how afraid are you? How much risk are you willing to take? Persons in sensitive occupations sometimes register a vehicle in a ficticious name, illegal as that may be. They get the ficticious name from a close friend or by acquiring documentation of another person's identification, such as a birth certificate of a deceased person. Once the vehicle has been registered in this person's name, a document is drawn up by a lawyer or a notary public, giving the person legal permission to drive it anywhere, in any state, for any purpose. This paper is carried in the glove compartment of the vehicle, in case there is a stop by local police and questioning about driving another's automobile. When renewing the registration, it is done by mail (if the state allows this) or by bringing in the same document used to register the car in the first place.

A legal and far more ethical way to distance yourself from your car's public information is to register it in a company or corporate name. The inexpensive method is to form a company, instead of a corporation, by obtaining a Doing Business As (DBA) certificate. Consult your local Chamber of Commerce representatives for how this is accomplished in your state. Once this company or corporation has been established and recorded, with you as either president, vice president, or secretary, you then register your automobile as belonging to this company. It becomes a "company car," not your personal vehicle. Where do you suppose this company is located? Well, it is at the same address where you receive your mail; it may even be the same box number. By the way, any private mailbox worth its salt will have mail-forwarding and a telephone answering service for its customers, another way to put distance between yourself and your real residence address and telephone number. To complete this protection of your privacy, have professionally designed and produced business cards made, listing the address and telephone number of your "mail drop," and if you are lucky, the FAX number of the private mailbox service. It's all an illusion, but an illusion that will go a long way in keeping questionable and dangerous characters from suddenly appearing at your doorstep.

Telephone numbers can be kept private, if you take the time to do it. Contact, in person, the local telephone company and ask to speak with a supervisor. Explain to this person that you have received death threats, or testified in court against an organized crime figure, or you are a successful bill collector and are hounded by those you found and made pay, or whatever your problem is, *discreetly* shared with this stranger. You must make him or her believe that your telephone number must be isolated and protected. Your story must be convincing. You won't get a second chance with the local telephone company. Complete the telephone company form for this purpose and annotate that you only give permission for the telephone company to release your home number to a bonafide police agency. *Also annotate that you request the telephone company to immediately notify you, at home or at work, when a police agency has requested your telephone number.* You would be surprised at the number of police officers, even those in supervisory positions, who make extra money by assisting local private investigators get information for which they are not legally entitled. Play it safe. We don't want to give police a bad rap. Most officers will not sell out a citizen. They, themselves, often are forced to "cover" where they live. They understand fear.

If you have gone to this much trouble to conceal your residence, you also should conceal your identity from others where you live. It is fairly easy for a good investigator to follow a person from work to his or her home, and then walk around, knocking on doors, checking mail boxes for names, asking for you (by name), and giving some cock-and-bull story why you must be contacted immediately ("She is coming into a sizable chunk of cash since a relative in Kansas just died; she has been selected as this year's Citizen of the Month, but her address cannot be ascertained, and the people at work want it to be a surprise to her; her mother is dying and she lost your address and phone number"; and other corny, but *workable*, lines). This way takes a little legwork but gets the job done.

Remove your name from your mailbox. If someone or some regulation prohibits thus, slightly deface it (by water, intense heat, etc.) so it is illegible, but not absolutely destroyed, for you do not want it replaced by a new, stronger name plate. Enter a Change of Address form at your local post office, rerouting all your mail from your residence to your new mail drop. Some post office branches are notoriously inefficient, so this process may have to be repeated each ninety days or whenever you notice delivery of mail addressed to you. Unfortunately, you cannot stop the delivery of junk mail, but since everyone gets reams of this each year, it is hard for a private investigator or a stalker to pinpoint which "resident" or "occupant" is you.

Tell your neighbors that you have an insane brother or ex-boyfriend whom you do not want to visit or have visit you and that he has been snooping around trying to find out where you live. No matter the story, it is important that your neighbors sympathize with you. Tell your neighbors not to tell anyone that you live there and to immediately let you know if someone asks for you.

Always park your car in a garage, no matter how temporarily you may be inside your home or how tired you are when you return home. All it takes is having the stalker who followed you home spot where your car is parked, and he or she is *really* warm. It is only a matter of time before your residence is known. All the stalker has to do is put your car under surveillance and wait for you to return, then back-track where you were seen coming from. If you don't have a garage, consider renting one from a nearby resident, advising the person you rent it from that absolutely no one is to know that you are the person renting it, again by using a cover story.

If a garage is not available, park your car one or two blocks away from your house, depending upon the weather, and walk, being careful who is around you, on foot or behind the wheel. Park in this same general spot each day, continuing the illusion that you live in one of the adjacent buildings. Park your car where the back license plate cannot be casually seen, such as close against a wall or another car. If your state requires that a vehicle has a license plate in front as well as the back, toss a small amount of mud on the front plate, or chewing gum on a torn sheet of paper, hidden just enough to make it unreadable. Most police officers won't become enraged if the front plate is soiled or bent, as long as you have one, but are more interested in the back plate, which shows registration periods and county of registration. The trick is to conceal your residence, not so much your vehicle. The vehicle, once identified as being driven by you, can lead the intruder to your home.

Be aware that voter registration information is available to just about anyone through proper channels. During the late Sixties, dissident groups obtained addresses and telephone numbers of police officers, items that had otherwise been protected through various means, to target them and their families for assassination. If you vote, use the address of the mail drop as your voting registration address. If your telephone number is requested, list your work phone number, saying that you don't have a home phone, since it is not a requirement to register. It is a simple thing to travel, once or twice a year, to wherever the voting poll is near your private mailbox service, and well worth the effort to protect your residence.

Don't forget mail order houses and magazine subscription files may carry your name and address, and they may sell mailing lists. Bear that in mind when ordering.

So, after all is said and done, if you have taken these precautions, what will be revealed to the person seeking to determine where you live. He or she will find that you are not listed by the telephone company, nor will you be found by tracing electrical, gas, or water records. Voter registration files will lead the investigator back to your mail drop. If he or she is able to get your mail drop information form, it will lead back to your work address and telephone. A check with local DMV files will turn up no vehicle registered to you, or at best, will reveal a vehicle registered to your fictitious company, whose address and telephone is the same as your private mailbox service. Should the investigator get lucky and be able to follow your company car to your neighborhood, nothing will be found by seeking information about a rented garage. You've done as much as you can to hide your residence from prying eyes.

The Achilles' heel in this process of covering yourself with anonymity is the chance that a stalker or private investigator will follow you from your work to your home. The usual answer to overcoming this problem is, "vary your route to and from home, watching for anyone following you." Simple, yet effective, but hard for the average, untrained citizen to do. Here are some tips:

1. Leave your residence and your work at different times, no matter what time you must report for work or end the day's business. Leave your home early or leave your work late, drive around, make many turns around blocks, drive through parking lots and behind supermarkets, places where no one else would be driving at that time and day. Watch what vehicle or vehicles continue to be behind you. After several turns around blocks, if you are being followed, you will be able to see the same vehicle behind you, making the same turns, and staying at the same speed. No matter how preposterous it seems, the person in that automobile is probably following you. If you do not see the same vehicle behind you after several turns, chances are slim that you are being followed.

2. If you *are* followed, you have two choices. You can try to lose the person following you (drive in such a way as to elude your follower), or you can drive to a police station and notify the police. For a person not schooled or experienced in "losing a tail," it is best to notify the police and seek their assistance. Do *not* stop and attempt to confront the person following you.

3. If you feel that passive security measures, such as those taken to protect your residence, are not enough, there are other ways to "harden the target." Bodyguards may be the answer. They are expensive, and you may not always get what you want. Even though these personal-protection "specialists" may cost you more than one-hundred-dollars per hour, they will not, in all probability, give their life for yours. There is a limit to their protection. And how effective are they, really?

In April 1992, former President Ronald Reagan was giving a speech on a stage in Las Vegas, having just received a 2-foot high, 30-pound crystal statue of an eagle. Suddenly a large man is standing beside him, having just shattered the eagle statue on the stage. He begins to say something but is immediately tackled by Secret Service agents and led from the area. The burly man, Richard Paul Springer, 41, could have injured or killed Reagan easily, rather than merely seeking a platform for a protest speech. Although the U.S. Secret Service is supposed to be the epitome of bodyguards, it was unable to stop a simple assault on a former president. If the Secret Service has this kind of trouble with the high-caliber agents it employs, government employees who *will* give their lives for their charge, what kind of similar service can you expect to find on the open market?

Realize that bodyguards are mainly useful to intimidate, to give the appearance of maximum security, to frighten the easily-scared, to provide a protective barrier between you and a perceived threat. This is about the extent of the protection you receive from bodyguards, be it one or fifty of them.

The key to protecting yourself is protective behavior, not protective barriers. Notwithstanding the fact that physical barriers, such as doors, windows, locks, lights, alarms, and other security devices are useful, all they do is slow the approach of a burglar or notify that an intruder is working his way into a protected area. By modifying behavior, you stand a better chance of not becoming a victim, of not placing yourself in vulnerable positions where you can be accosted, injured, or robbed.

IF YOU ARE STALKED

Stalkers are obsessive people. They can be acquaintances, former lovers or a person you have never met. Many stalkers will "hound" a victim for years, and until recently, victims lived restrained, very tense lives because there were no laws harsh enough to handle stalkers adequately. Stalkers could be repeatedly arrested by police, but punishment was so weak, there was no deterrent against the crime. Too often stalkers were told merely to stay away, or police didn't take the crime seriously.

If someone follows you, harasses you and makes a *credible* threat of bodily injury or death, you can get the help you need to stop a stalker. The key word is "credible." Many stalkers are crafty and intelligent. They conduct their crimes very skillfully, slithering through the loopholes in the stalking laws. What should you do if a stalker is bothering you, and he or she has found where you live? First, get a restraining order. This puts on public record that you are being harassed. After you get the restraining order, call the police about every infraction of the stalker. Every one, every day and every night, if it is necessary. This allows police to track the stalker's behavior. Make sure police reports are filed, that information is documented. Do not talk to the stalker, do not acknowledge that he or she is there, is bothering you, or that there is any significance to their presence. Stalkers look for victims' reactions. Don't give them the satisfaction. Can a stalker end up hurting you? Yes. Stalkers have killed their victims. This crime should be taken seriously. A stalker is not a stable person.

All states do not have stalking laws. The following do: California, Colorado, Connecticut, Delaware, Florida, Hawaii, Idaho, Iowa, Kentucky, Massachussets, Mississippi, Nebraska, Oklahoma, South Carolina, South Dakota, Tennessee, Utah, Virginia, Washington, West Virginia and Wisconsin. If your state is not listed, contact your state representative or your state attorney general for his or her support in establishing a stalking law.

35

Protective Potpourri

LIGHTS AND LIGHTING

Light your ADDRESS AT NIGHT so police or an emergency vehicle can see it easily.

A MOTION LIGHT can light walkways for the safety of friends, while they will startle burglars and make them take routes they do not prefer.

The BEST PLACE FOR OUTDOOR LIGHTS is beneath eaves. They should be high enough that an intruder cannot unscrew the bulbs.

Buy an AUTOMATIC TIMER that will turn the lights on at dusk and off at dawn. As the days grow longer, or with DAYLIGHT SAVINGS TIME, do not delay in adjusting the timer. A burglar looks for that "window" of days, when home owners simply don't get to the task of changing a timer's hours.

Photosensitive lights that switch on and off in response to existing light are better. When a storm makes the yard particularly dark, earlier than usual, you won't have to worry. The light sensors will do the thinking for you. Even when you aren't at home, the yard will be lighted. Do not locate lights near vegetation that affects their timing, such as placing them in the shade of bushes or branches.

It is a good idea, if you live in a high-crime area, to protect outdoor lights with a rock-resistant cover—transparent plastic with a wire mesh.

If you are going to install special security lighting outside, and will have television monitoring on your grounds, it is best

to hire a certified security consultant for advice on can-
dlepower, camera and light restrictions, and other influences
about which the lay person may be unaware.

WINDOWS

One of the worst security hazards in your home is the
window air conditioner. It is possible to better protect the home
by replacing the weak side-panels, normally provided by the air
conditioner manufacturer upon purchase, with strong wood or
steel pieces.

Ensure that your window air conditioner is security
mounted on L-frames on the outside of the home and that the
L-frames are tightly connected by long screws or bolts to the
window frame. Connections to the window frame should be on
both sides of the window, inside and outside.

The transoms (old-fashioned windows over doors) in your
home should be permanently secured in a way that prohibits a
human body from moving through them. If the transom is used
for ventilation, then merely secure the window frame in a permanently open position, but with a slight aperture.

Locking a SLIDING GLASS DOOR while it is partly open,
is not advisable. A strong intruder with a crowbar will be able
to pry it open. Sliding glass doors can be lifted out of their
tracks, through the use of a screwdriver.

One window in a bedroom on each level of your house
should be designated as your FIRE EXIT during an emergency.
Guests in your home should be told of this exit. Iron grillwork or
bars should not be used on bedroom windows unless they open
from the inside.

Glazing windows makes them shatter-resistent. Check
your windows to ensure that window putty has been placed on
the inside of the windows and not just on the outside. There are
skilled burglars who excell in quickly removing exterior putty,
and the entire glass with it, for quiet entry into homes.

Louvered windows and panes invite burglars and intruders. Louvered windows should be immediately replaced. If
replacement is not possible, the individual louvers should be
glued in place, preventing the panes from being removed by
sliding out. Use epoxy only.

If your window can be closed or opened by a hand-crank,

remove the lever handle after use. This prevents the accidental opening of a window, or the manipulation of the handle to fully open the window through a partial opening.

FLASHLIGHT

For use in emergencies, purchase an INDUSTRIAL FLASHLIGHT. They use Krypton bulbs, which are nearly 70 percent brighter and illuminate an area far wider than an ordinary bulb. Prices range from ten-dollars and up.

If you suspect an intruder, do *not* try to handle things yourself. And, *if* you are using a flashlight to get through your yard or your home during dangerous times, hold the light *away* from your body, as police are trained to do. That way, if an intruder targets the light, there is a good chance, he will miss you.

VALUABLES

Place jewelry, handguns and other smaller valuable on a dark blue towel, take a photograph. If these items are stolen, you can reclaim them with the picture. Otherwise, if they are recovered, they will be sold at an annual police auction.

DO NOT allow a DOOR-TO-DOOR VENDOR to VIDEO-TAPE your valuables. He may be a thief using this method to "case" what you have with intention to return later and steal your property.

Maintain an up-to-date LIST of the SERIAL NUMBERS of all electronic appliances, cars, firearms, motorcycles, etc. Keep one list at home and another at the office for extra security. LIST, with detailed descriptions, all valuables which do not have serial numbers. Keep two such lists at different locations, for security.

Inscribe your driver's license number on your television, recorders and other expensive items. Most police departments will loan such engravers, or a crime prevention officer will make a house call to assist you in engraving your social security or driver license number on your valuables.

The DREMEL ELECTRIC ENGRAVER permanently marks metal, wood, plastic, ceramic and other common surfaces. A calibrated stroke adjustment dial controls engraving depth. Diamond tips are available for extremely hard surfaces. SETEN IDENTIFICATION PRODUCTS.

The SECURIKIT, available through Seten, uses ULTRA-VIOLET MARKING. It permanently identifies your equipment. Markings can be identified only through ultraviolet light. The kit has two ultraviolet pens, one fine point and one thick point. A portable UV light, with batteries included, warning tags and a carrying case are part of the kit.

Another identifying instrument brands tools. Your address or driver's license number can be burned into wood, plastics, wood and even your new leather chair or briefcase. Cost is less than two hundred dollars. It comes in 125 watts up to 300 watts, depending upon degree of usage and the size of the wording in your brand. Available through Seten distributors.

GRAFFITI REMOVER

GRAFFITTI REMOVER sprays on as a jelly. The cleaning agents penetrate the markings. After a few minutes, you simply wipe away the mess. It cleans off spray paint, marking pens, crayons, lipstick, ball point ink, and more. It is advertised as safe on steel, aluminum, fiberglass, baked enamel, procelain, ceramic tile, formica, brick, concrete and glass. It should *not* be used on beaded signs. The Seten company claims one can will erase over 100 markings. Price less than fifteen dollars per can.

INVITING TROUBLE

Putting your NAME ON YOUR DOORMAT or on a decorative address plate may be chic, but it invites trouble. It allows burglars, or worse, to know your name. They can go to a phone booth and will call your name by looking for the address that matches it, to see if you are home. If no one answers, or a child or daughter takes the call, you have invited trouble. Don't give strangers information, especially on an elaborate sign where you live.

36

The Ultimate Break-In: War in the Streets Can You Prepare?

In a society convulsing with change, the central need . . . is for far more sensitive information—especially anticipatory information—about the environment in which one must function. This information must go beyond economics. It is important to know about social stresses, potential crisis, shifts in population, changes in family structure, political upheavals and to know about these early enough, to make adaptive decisions.

Alvin Toffler

Author of *Futureshock*

Even prior to the Los Angeles riots of the summer of 1992, the most frequent question asked of us, was "when the riots come, how can we protect ourselves?" From respected criminologists, police officers who work the streets, and social scientists alike, there are predictions of massive civil unrest during the Nineties. These predictions came long before the L. A. riots and copy-cat disturbances in other American cities in May of '92. A riot poses the "ULTIMATE THREAT OF BREAK-IN" and is akin to war in the streets, the most frightening experience citizens or police can face.

Although the Federal Bureau of Investigation is traditionally very conservative, America has been conservatively governed for almost twelve years; the FBI has disseminated startling projections of massive civil unrest in the Nineties to chiefs of police across the nation. The projections are *grounded in science*, and that is what makes them so unsettling. The "point person" for the studies is Dr. William Tafoya, an FBI agent for 17 years, with a Master's Degree from USC and a doctorate in criminology from the University of Maryland. Tafoya used to be a police officer, before joining the FBI, and was a faculty member of the FBI Academy for 11 years, assigned to the Behavioral Science Instruction and Research Unit. He taught a course on long-range planning for police and computer-based forecasting. His exhaustive computer studies, on everything from homeless children to violence associated with drugs, are pretty scary. All Americans, especially those living in cities, near interstate highways and in major poverty pockets of the nation, should be aware of what police management already knows. The projections are that crime will continue to escalate and become more violent as we approach 1999, at which time, the lid may blow off the nation.

The predicted scenario—minorities, claiming their lot hasn't improved in over twenty years, pitted against middle-class whites who are angry over economic breaks for minorities, which they perceive as being granted at their expense. David Carter, professor of criminal justice at Michigan State University, believes the casualties will be very high because America is now so heavily armed. The predicted civil unrest will be a combination of class and race war.

FBI behavioral scientist Dr. Tafoya, says that, "If it is not probably, it is a strong possibility that the poor and blacks will be driving through white-collar neighborhoods shooting and robbing and looting. It will be an act of desperation and rage. Once the poor invade suburbia, the yuppies are going to arm themselves and start a vigilante movement." By 1995, acts of political terrorism in America are projected to increase by more than 50 percent over the 1985 level. The causes?

From 1978 to 1985, the number of poor households jumped by more than 25 percent, while the number of low-rent housing units dropped by 20 percent. Drug related arrests jumped by 126 percent from 1980 to 1989. The homicide rate among black males 15 to 24 years-old in 1987 was 85.6 times per 100,000, more than seven times that of white males. Poor and minorities, who once believed they could look to government for hope and leadership to make the economy better for everyone, now feel abandoned by the super-rich. T. H. Poole, Sr., president of Florida's NAACP, said that when citizens can't control anything, they lose control. While community policing may help a little, it will not be a solution, according to Dr. Tafoya and other scholars. The causes of the future civil unrest are too overwhelming. Tafoya calls it, "The Witches Brew." When the Los Angeles riots occurred, Dr. Tafoya told us that he had telephone calls from all over the world, reporters telling him, "I know . . . you told us so." To which he replied, "No, this isn't it. It's still coming."

Can you prepare for what is predicted? We asked the question of security experts, some of the country's top police officers, and security architects who specialize in designing fortresses.

Sergeant Richard Doyle of the Boston Police Department was in the 1966 riots. He laughed about the attitude of some police officers who watched the 1992 Los Angeles riots on television and had quick answers to stemming civil unrest."Let me tell you something," Doyle said. "You don't ever want to be in a riot. You really don't. I changed my pants more than once a day, during the riots." If people are going from block to block, fire-bombing and dragging people out of cars, Doyle says, "Under no circumstances, go out. Riots start off with people frustrated, then they get into the looting. Most of the people out there aren't into destroying property" as much as taking what they can take. If you're in a riot, you'll have a problem if you are in a liquor store. Chances are, you won't be attacked in your home. Residences over stores, near or attached to stores, have been of greatest risks during riots." However, Doyle says a lot of crimes unrelated to riots occur during riots. "They're having a problem with their next door neighbor two doors down, or young kids are raising Caine, and they're always complaining about it, and then the riot begins. They can retaliate during the riot and blame it on the riot. If people are firebombing close by," Doyle says, "get out. Go to the next house, or the next, for protection. You're pretty much on your own during a riot."

Caution: Sergeant Doyle speaks of the traditional Sixties-style of civil disturbance. The projected unrest during the Nineties is supposed to be more violent, is supposed to last longer, and there may not be enough federal troops in the United States to bring it under control. Additionally, the money available to curb lengthy civil disobedience twenty years ago will be absent in the Nineties. The range of problems now goes beyond civil rights difficulties. Drugs and gangs are two elements that dramatically worsen mob violence.

Gangs use firebombs to intimidate, and they are also a favorite tool of destruction during civil unrest. According to architect Jeff Sulkin, even if you have the money to have sprinklers throughout your home, they will not protect you against firebombing. (The problem with sprinklers is two-fold. Sprinkler water can do as much damage as fire or smoke damage.) If you live in a region with heightened danger of civil unrest (or your vacation home is on Israel's West Bank), you may want a home made of concrete with doors made of metal, which is grained to look like wood. Thermal glass, which is normally for radiation control, also can insulate against the heat of fire, at least, for a period of time, depending on the thickness of the glass and the glazing. Flashing will be one of the most important components in a home protected against rioting and firebombs.

Flashing is a piece of metal. There are 200 kinds. Flashing allows an overlap between a piece of window-frame and the wall it is touching. It bends up between the wood, behind the concrete, or it's bolted to a steel rivet. It is a transition piece in construction. Properly applied, flashing prevents water from penetrating, and it can also prevent gasoline from Molotov cocktails from going through to the inside of a house. According to Sulkin, "Anyone who does proper window flashing on all windows, in copper or noncorrosive material, drastically limits fire-born chemicals from getting through. It *is* possible to build a riot-proof house."

Having a pipeline out to the rest of a city or region during civil unrest makes many people feel more secure. Granted, the police will be so busy, they may not be able to respond, but a cellular telephone is a tremendous security tool simply because it allows communication at all. Another article that can make your life easier during such a disaster: a pocket-sized battery-powered television. Black-and-white sets retail for about one-hundred dollars. A battery-powered radio is important gear, and don't forget to have extra batteries on hand. Spare batteries can be left in the refrigerator for longer life.

If you are not yet at the center of mob violence, but the violence and burning is coming in your direction, you can vacate. Be careful not to drive through or near potential flash-points. Carry an "earthquake" kit in your car, containing medical supplies, sleeping bags, water, flashlight and batteries, food, and a small tent. If you have room, add a lawn chair and a TV tray and don't forget toilet paper. Whether or not you carry a weapon is up to you.

Police usually can predict when a riot is ready to happen. If you read your newspapers carefully, you also may know when bad times are close. Look for inflammatory language on the part of civic leaders and social and political activists. Watch for an approaching "trigger event." Look for large thefts or bur-glaries of ammunition stores, construction firms (explosives) and sporting goods stores (rifles, pistols, ammunition, survival gear). The articles in the newspaper describing these events may be small, but they are significant.

How far are we, as a society, willing to go to be safe? Are we not looking at handling a growing crime problem *after* the fact? Are better and stronger locks, windows and doors the answer to living defensively, or is changing behavior a better, less expensive answer? Twenty sets of human eyes in a neighborhood, trained to observe knowledgeably, are far better than a security system that may malfunction. Education, good parenting, knowing your neighbors and building a network in the community can stem the tide of crime. Police have found that tutoring of young males in junior high school and high school coursework remarkably lowers a community's burglary rate.

The FBI's Dr. Tafoya recommends reaching out to those who are different, *not* having a separatism between ethnic groups, religious groups, and economic groups. Work with minority youth, especially the males. Have your police agency review its riot control plans. Tolerate diversity.

It is alarming that with each crime or instance of violent civil unrest comes even greater separatism, which, in turn, winds the spring tighter. Do what you can to make your "home your castle," but if you are truly concerned about crime, begin investing in a more balanced society for all Americans. No wall is high enough to keep out an army of the bitter, well-armed, underclass who gave up on the system. Correcting the social ills that contribute to crime and violence is the least expensive and most caring route to making your home a safe place.

If your city has pockets of despair and extreme poverty, an

effort must be made now to emphasize community policing. Install officers with sensitivity to that despair in sub-stations, where citizens can directly approach the police for help. Every opportunity must be used to diffuse the tension building toward the fateful year when "The Witches Brew" of drugs, violence, homelessness, and joblessness boils over.

37

If You Are
a Victim . . .

If you are a victim of a crime, *during* that crime try to memorize descriptions that can help the police—height, weight, hair and eye color, clothing, type of weapon used, and distinguishing characteristics of your assailant. When the police dispatcher answers, report that you are victim of a (your) crime. Give your location, then your name. Tell the dispatcher if you need medical help. Describe the assailant and any weapons.

If you are sexually assaulted, do *not* bathe afterwards, *or* douche, *or* change clothes. Get to a doctor within 12 hours of the attack for a medical examination. Do *not* clean your house after a crime. *Don't touch anything*—it may be evidence. Call the police or dial 911. Report *all* crimes. It is your responsibility to society.

It is normal to feel guilty, helpless and lonely; it is OK to cry. Victims often endure severe psychological and financial problems as a result of a crime. If a suspect is caught, victims, along with suspects, usually face legal difficulties.

The victims' activist movement has been very successful in recent years. There are citizens' self-help groups, associations and public assistance monies for crime victims, with some states offering financial compensation to victims. Victims also can request restitution from the person who commits the crime. Parole agents and police often encourage it. If the perpetrator of your crime has property or a job, it may be worth your while to sue.

If you cannot afford an attorney, call the local bar association for information about legal aid. If you *can* afford a lawyer, do not find one in the yellow pages. The yellow pages can be a start, but in this game you should not gamble. Beware of lawyers who show up on your doorstep to help you. If you call your county bar association, they may not recommend a specific attorney even if you beg. They are not allowed to play one lawyer off against another because they represent all members of the association.

A clue to an attorney's background can be found in a book of practicing lawyers, published by the state bar association, usually found at your local library. In California, it's called the *Parker Guide.* Ask for the reference librarian's help. Find out how long after graduation an attorney passed the bar exam. If an attorney worked at other jobs for three years after graduation, he may have flunked the bar exams and bounced around awhile. Look for clues to his success. He may carry a very expensive briefcase, but he never cleans his teeth and he doesn't own a filing cabinet. When finding a lawyer, it is *very* important that you give yourself a few days to shop around.

Finally, a warning: The wrong attorney can complicate your life terribly. In our work with crime and police, we have observed a phenomenon. Unstable people often flock to crime victims because they enjoy the excitement and drama that surrounds them. That group can include lawyers, who have a perfect excuse to be close to the eye of the storm. These individuals will thrive on the complications and whirlwind that surround you; they will make themselves the center of attention with the press, and they may eventually place emotion on a higher priority than legal scholarship. Beware. That is *not* what you need.

When you have your first meeting with an attorney, there is usually no charge. Find out in advance. Ask how long the attorney has been at the firm. Look around. If he keeps his files in a cardboard box next to his desk, and he's allegedly a successful lawyer with several years experience, beware. Remember, lawyers have different specialties, just like doctors. A bankruptcy lawyer may not serve you well on your rape or assault case, but he or she may not divulge this deficiency, especially if it means the difference between getting a retainer fee from you or not getting it.

You will be advised about the time period under which you must file a lawsuit, an appropriate court that will hear the case, and about collecting the judgement. If you want restitution from the criminal, contact the distict attorney or prosecuting attorney who is handling the case. You can do that yourself. This attorney may push for what you desire or at least make your requests known to the court.

Awards from the state not covered by insurance or damages awarded from a lawsuit can include what you spent on medical care and psychological counseling, on funeral and burial expenses, job training and lost income, all costs you incurred as a result of the crime. You may be eligible for such awards: if you were injured as a result of a crime; if the victim of the crime was your financial support; or if you are a family member of the victim and you need counseling to deal with the crime.

In order to gain monies that may be available after victimization, you must cooperate with the police in the investigation and prosecution of the case, and your *own* behavior must not have contributed to the crime. Lost property usually is not covered by public monies.

Citizens' groups that can help you deal with the aftermath of victimization include Parents of Murdered Children, The National Organization for Victim Assistance, Mothers Against Drunk Drivers (MADD), and the National Victim Center. The Victims of Crime Resource Center in Sacramento, California, at the McGeorge School of Law, has a toll-free number: 1 (800) VICTIMS. The Victims of Crime Resource Center offers a federally funded study of victims' participation in sentencing and parole and shares up-to-date information regarding restitution and other victims' matters.

If you think surviving the crime is the worst of your suffering, brace yourself. Going through a trial is no picnic. Take it from one who knows. The following was written for this book by Ala Auersperg Isham, co-founder with her brother, Alexander, of the National Victim Center, headquartered in Arlington, Virginia.

"People think a victim's nightmare ends when the attack is over. But, the nightmare is only beginning. For victims and their family, the shock and pain of what they may face at the hands of our criminal justice system, can be as painful as the shock of being mugged or raped, or having a loved one murdered. They may suffer untold emotional grief, financial hardship, and public humiliation, only to watch the offender become the center of attention, in a legal system that goes to great lengths to protect the rights of the criminal.

"My brother, Alex, and I started the National Victim Center to help spearhead the fight for rights of victims of violent crimes. The center connects victims with providers of care, service and assistance, and helps grassroots organizations develop quality programs to help victims. Victims of violent crimes need special emotional and legal counseling. That's why the Victim Center exists."

Ala Auersperg Isham

(Daughter of Sunny von Bulow)

38

Security and
Protection Resources

Handgun Control
1225 Eye Street NW
Suite 1100
Washington, DC 20005

Weapons issues.

Cyro Canada, Inc.
360 Carlingview Drive
Etobicoke, Ontario,
Canada M 9W 5X9
(800) 461-7398

Acrylic and polycarbonate
sheets. Building codes
should be followed closely
when using these materi-
als. They are toxic when
burned.

Fortner Custom Doors
3186 East La Palma Avenue
Anaheim, CA 92806
(714) 630-0770

International sales outlet
for custom and security
doors and accessories. Emphasize security aspect of
inquiry when calling or
writing.

National Rifle Association
1600 Rhode Island
Avenue NW
Washington, DC 20006
(800) 368-5714

Gun safety and firearms
control issues.

Gandall Safe Corporation
(800) 722-7233

Information on safes, including custom-built containers. Call for local vendor addresses and information.

The Safety Zone
2515 East 43rd Street
Box 182247
Chattanooga, TN 37422-7247
(800) 999-3030

Absolute cornucopia of security and protection products; "The Jammer," "Phone Home" (device that allows a child to call home collect, even if he doesn't know the number), super peepholes, gun locks, and other clever and innovative products.

MAG Home Security
Products
13711 Alma Avenue
Gardena, CA 90249

Home security products—door strike plates, deadbolts, door strengtheners.

Wright and Associates
1000 Victor's Way
Suite 300
Ann Arbor, MI 48108

Security expert Jerry Wright, CPP. Recommended as a professional by American Society for Industrial Security (ASIS).

National Institute of
Dog Training
1839 Portrero Grande Drive
Monterey Park, CA 91754
(818) 571-4900

Mathew Margolis, Owner and Trainer. Dog training techniques.

Master Animal Care
Lake Road
Mountaintop, PA 18707-0330
(800) 346-0749

Amazing number of dog
care products, including, a
concrete pile of dog drop-
pings, to hide your keys in
out in the yard. Looks ex-
ceptionally real.

Conley Security Agency
550 Saddlery Building
309 Court Avenue
Des Moines, IA 50309

John H. Conley, CPP.
Recommended as a profes-
sional by the American Society for Industrial Security (ASIS).

Textured Coatings of
America
5950 South Avalon Blvd.
Los Angeles, CA 90003-1384

Graffiti Guard products.

National Center for
Missing and
Exploited Children
2101 Wilson Blvd.
Suite 550
Arlington, VA 22201-3052
(800) 843-5678

Advice and publications on
missing and exploited
children.

Long Beach Uniform
Company
2789 Long Beach Blvd.
Long Beach, CA 90806
(310) 424-0220

Police and security equipment, uniforms, and pub-
lications. Major supplier
for the greater Los Angeles
area police.

National Victim Center
309 West 7th Street
Suite 709
Fort Worth, TX 76102
(817) 877-3355

Victim information, coun-
seling and publications.

Pet Alert
P.O. Box 1690-B
Garden Grove, CA 92642

Pet protection kit, "In Case of Emergency, Please Locate and Save My Pet(s)."

International Association of
Chiefs of Police
1110 North Glebe Road
Suite 200
Arlington, VA 22201

Current information on law enforcement policies, police technology, equipment, professional issues, and publications.

Dan Weedon
Licensed Security
Landscape Architect
8500 Melrose Avenue
Suite 205 A
West Hollywood, CA 90069

Contemporary information on all aspects of security landscaping.

Sulkin and Associates
1748 Berkeley Street
Santa Monica, CA 90404

Jeff Sulkin, Architect. Professional security design and "high end" residence architecture.

Seton Identification Products
P.O. Box FJ-1331
New Haven, CT 06505
(800) 243-6624

Ultra-violet Security Marking Systems
Engravers, Electronic Branding Tools, Simulated Surveillance Cameras, and more.

The Sharper Image
650 Davis Street
San Francisco, CA 94111
(800) 344-4444

Up-scale dog products. Features "The Shadowmaker," which simulates people's movement in an empty house, and other privacy-protection products.

Products, services, and advice provided by those entities, companies, and individual personnel listed herein are the sole responsibility of those people dispensing, selling, leasing, or otherwise dealing with customers, clientele, and readers soliciting information, products, or advice. The authors make no claim of fact, responsibility, or endorsement of any person, product or service in this publication, but only identify products and capabilities and describe particular methods, mechanics, and usages.